How to Attract
and Keep
Active Church Members

Also by Donald P. Smith

Congregations Alive

How to Attract
and Keep
Active Church Members

Donald P. Smith

Westminster/John Knox Press
Louisville, Kentucky

Scripture quotations are from the New Revised Standard Version of the Bible, copyright © 1989 by the Division of Christian Education of the National Council of the Churches of Christ in the U.S.A., and are used by permission.

Book design by Kevin Raquepaw

First edition

Published by Westminster/John Knox Press
Louisville, Kentucky

This book is printed on acid-free paper that meets the American National Standards Institute Z39.48 standard.∞

PRINTED IN THE UNITED STATES OF AMERICA

9 8 7 6 5 4 3 2 1

Library of Congress Cataloging-in-Publication Data

Smith, Donald P., 1922–
    How to attract and keep active church members / Donald P. Smith.— 1st ed.
        p.   cm.
    Includes bibliographical references and index.
    ISBN 0-664-25140-4 (pbk. : alk. paper)
     1. Church growth—United States. 2. Church membership—United States. 3. Church renewal. 4. Public relations—Churches. 5. Presbyterian Church (U.S.A.)—History—20th century. 6. Ex-church members—United States—Presbyterian Church. 7. Commitment to the church. I. Title.
   BR526.S595 1992
   254'.5—dc20   92-9495

CONTENTS

PREFACE

The ideas in this book come from many sources. For thirty-five years I have worked closely with ordained ministers and lay church professionals. They have taught me about styles of pastoral leadership that encourage congregational vitality. During the research and writing of two books, I have learned much from many.

Clergy in the Cross Fire (1973) dealt with role conflict and ambiguity in the ministry. Chapter 8 contains some of its insights. *Congregations Alive* (1981) was a study of ninety-seven congregations in which members actively minister to one another and to the community. We compared questionnaires from pastors and elders of those "ministering congregations" with a scientific random sample of Presbyterian pastors and elders in the Presbyterian Panel.[1] In that study, I interviewed scores of people who have made a lasting impact on my life. Some of their insights occur throughout this book. They are identified in the text by a reference to "ministering congregations."

Following publication of *Congregations Alive,* we compared skill ratings of the pastors of the ministering congregations with skill ratings of the Presbyterian Panel. We then met with the ministering pastors to learn about the life experiences that had shaped their styles of ministry. Chapter 13 contains some of our conclusions.

The bulk of this book grows out of a study of church growth and membership retention. Based on a review of the literature, I formulated nine hypotheses to describe churches that would be effective in retaining their members. These appear in my essay "Closing the Back Door" in *The Mainstream Protestant "Decline": The Presbyterian Pattern,* published by Westminster/John Knox Press in 1990. With permission of the book's editors, Milton J Coalter, John M. Mulder, and Louis B. Weeks, I have made extensive use of that material throughout this book. When I say "studies have found . . . ," or words to that effect, readers can find documentation in that essay.[2]

To simplify the gathering and analysis of data, we conducted the balance of the study with Presbyterian churches. Accordingly, this book often uses Presbyterian terminology. However, I am confident that the findings apply to other denominations. The reader should translate "session" to read "official board" or other congregational governing group. Translate "presbytery" to "district conference" or other regional judicatory.

Six hundred churches completed questionnaires based on the nine hypotheses. Two hundred ninety-eight of them had the highest rates of membership loss in the Presbyterian Church (U.S.A.) over a five-year period (we did not include losses through death or transfer of membership). We call those congregations "high-loss churches." The other 302 congregations had the lowest rates of loss over the same period. We call them "bonding churches." There were three different questionnaires: one for pastors, a second for a session committee, and a third for up to four selected members who were not on the session. We calculated statistical differences between the questionnaire responses from high-loss churches and bonding churches.

We had average fall Sunday attendance estimates from 415 churches. Ignoring rates of membership loss, we found that roughly half those churches had an average attendance equivalent to 50 percent or more of their membership. Half had attendance rates less than 50 percent of their membership. We call those congregations "high-attendance" and "low-attendance" churches, respectively.

Of the 433 churches studied from the perspective of size, 238 (55 percent) had a membership of two hundred or less; 128 (30 percent) had between 201 and five hundred members; 67 (15 percent) had 501 members or more. We refer to those churches as "small," "medium," and "large."

As expected, some congregations with low rates of loss (the bonding churches) had been lax in clearing their rolls of members who had dropped out of congregational life. To correct for this problem, we decided to repeat our analysis with modified samples. We removed from the revised samples, bonding churches that had reviewed their membership rolls less than once every two years. In addition we made several other minor changes so that the high-loss and bonding samples would contain a more nearly proportionate number of small, medium, and large churches. The new statistical analyses of these refined samples resulted in very few changed results. Therefore, in this book, we have used both the original analysis and the analysis of the refined samples.

Whenever we say "our study found . . . ," we refer to the results of this questionnaire analysis at a .05 level of statistical significance.[3]

Our study of bonding churches concluded with on-site interviews in eighteen congregations. My wife, Verna, and I interviewed more than two hundred people. In addition I interviewed many other pastors and lay leaders on the telephone. Most of the illustrative material comes from those interviews. In some cases I have combined quotations from several pastors or members into a composite quotation. I have edited some for brevity or clarity.

Except when mentioned in an endnote, the names of churches and individuals are fictitious.

Within the scope of this study, it was not possible to interview dropouts from either the high-loss or the bonding churches. I depend upon other studies for whatever insights I have on reasons for dropping out.

Reference throughout the book to the *Membership Trends* study is to a 1976 study of church membership trends in the United Presbyterian Church in the U.S.A.[4]

A bonanza of information on faith maturity emerged from the monumental 1990 study *Effective Christian Education,* funded by the Lilly Endowment. The project involved six major denominations.

> One of the most important findings in this study is that congregations effective in promoting faith maturity reap the benefit of greater loyalty. By concentrating on their ultimate purpose of nurturing an ongoing growth in faith, congregations appear to gain the kind of commitment that thwarts dropout, switching, and inactivity.[5]

The following conclusions from that study might well have been written to describe the bonding churches in our study:

> In congregational life, people learn the faith in a variety of ways. Often it comes through informal patterns of interaction. Thus we note that warmth, caring, and service, in combination, contribute to growth and loyalty. . . .
>
> Since family, friends, service, and receiving care are all important for promoting faith, programming efforts to increase these experiences will pay rich dividends. These efforts might include teaching parents skills necessary to promote the faith of children, teaching adults and youth how to show care and concern to others, and introducing meaningful structured opportunities to serve others.[6]

Thanks are due to many people without whose interest and cooperation this book never would have been possible. John M. Mulder, Louis Weeks, and Milton J Coalter, Jr., made available Lilly Endowment funding for writing the initial essay. This encouraged me to initiate the project. I thank them also for permission to use material from that essay.

The Evangelism and Church Development Ministry Unit of the Presbyterian Church (U.S.A.) provided the funding for the questionnaire studies and on-site visits. In particular I want to thank its two directors. Patricia M. Roach first caught the vision of the possibilities in this study. She secured the unit's backing for the project. Andrea E. Pfaff succeeded her as director of the unit. Not only did she give enthusiastic support to the project, she also made many helpful suggestions. Julianne Jens-Horton handled the details of administrative liaison with the unit. Gary Demarest gave his encouragement and recommended several congregations with effective programs for single young adults.

The Office of Research of the denomination did a masterful job of collecting and analyzing voluminous data through innumerable computer studies. In particular, I am deeply indebted to Arthur Benjamin for his perceptive professional guidance and direction of the research process. Ida Smith deserves a special word of thanks for her meticulous programming. She was cheerfully available at every point in the process. Patiently and promptly she produced accurate additional data whenever I asked for it.

My wife, Verna, and I are grateful to W. Ben Lane and the Education and Congregational Nurture Ministry Unit of the Presbyterian Church (U.S.A.) for making it possible for us to attend the conference that interpreted the *Effective Christian Education* study.

Of course I cannot forget the pastors and sessions of six hundred congregations that participated in the study. Thanks go to the thousands of members who took the time to complete questionnaires, some of which were rather lengthy. In particular I am grateful for the pastors and church officers whose anonymous insights I have used throughout the book.

In conclusion special thanks go to Verna, my partner in life and colleague in this study. She patiently endured my long hours at the computer keyboard. Her advice at many points was invaluable. And her skillful interviewing and careful note-taking has added much detail to the descriptions in this book.

Rarely is there a truly original idea. Perhaps there are a few in this book. But most, in some way, come from others, many of whom I cannot remember or do not even know. Of those whom I do know, it is impossible to identify all their insights or to give them adequate credit. I hope that those who are not mentioned will forgive this shortcoming. Thanks then go to the many who, in interaction with me over the years, have generated what for me have been fresh insights.

ACKNOWLEDGMENTS

Quotations from Lyle E. Schaller, *Assimilating New Members,* copyright © 1978 by Lyle E. Schaller, used by permission of Abingdon Press.

Quotations from John Ackerman, "Cherishing our Differences: Personality Types in the Church," in *Action Information* 12, no. 2 (March/April 1986), p. 17, used by permission from The Alban Institute, Inc. 4125 Nebraska Avenue, NW, Washington, DC 20016. Copyright 1986. All rights reserved.

Quotations from Donald P. Smith, *Clergy in the Cross Fire,* copyright © 1973 by Westminster Press, used by permission of Westminster/John Knox Press.

Quotations from Donald P. Smith, *Congregations Alive,* copyright © 1981 by Westminster Press, used by permission of Westminster/John Knox Press.

Quotations from C. Ellis Nelson, *Congregations: Their Power to Form and Transform,* © copyright John Knox Press 1988. Used by permission of Westminster/John Knox Press.

Quotations from the videotapes *Coping with Conflict* are used by permission of the Synod of Lakes and Prairies, Presbyterian Church (U.S.A.).

Quotations from Robert Gribbon, *Developing Faith in Young Adults,* used by permission from the Alban Institute, Inc., 4125 Nebraska Avenue, NW, Washington, DC 20016. Copyright 1990. All rights reserved.

Material from Speed B. Leas, *Discover Your Conflict Management Style,* used by permission from The Alban Institute, Inc., 4125 Nebraska Avenue, NW, Washington, DC 20016. Copyright 1984. All rights reserved.

Quotations from Peter L. Benson and Carolyn Eklin, *Effective Christian Education: A National Study of Protestant Congregations—A Summary Report,* copy-

Acknowledgments

Quotations from the Shipmates leaflet (n.d.) are used by permission of the Rev. Mary Graves.

Quotations from *U.S. Lifestyles and Mainline Churches: A Key to Reaching People in the 90's,* by Tex Sample, © 1990 Tex Sample. Used by permission of Westminster/John Knox Press.

Material from John S. Savage, *Why Active Members Stay Active,* videotape, copyright © 1987 by L.E.A.D. Consultants, Inc., used by permission.

Quotations from *The Work of the Minister of Youth,* edited and revised by Richard Ross, copyright © 1989 by Convention Press. Used by permission.

Quotations from Henri J. M. Nouwen, *The Wounded Healer: Ministry in Contemporary Society,* copyright © 1972 by Doubleday & Company, Inc., used by permission.

Quotations from Jolene L. Roehlkepartain, *Youth Ministry: Its Impact on Church Growth,* are used by permission of Group Publishing, Box 481, Loveland, CO 80539.

INTRODUCTION

Said the queen to Alice, "Now, *here*, you see, it takes all the running *you* can do, to keep in the same place. If you want to get somewhere else, you must run at least twice as fast as that!"

LEWIS CARROLL, *THROUGH THE LOOKING-GLASS*[1]

H elp!" cried the head of the membership committee. "It's worse than a treadmill! The faster we run, the further behind we get. We have a good evangelism and member-recruitment program. A parade of people comes in the front door. Then before we realize it, they drift out the back. We have even lost some of our old faithfuls. They've just dropped out! What can we do?"

A cry like this could well arise from thousands of congregations. Most mainline denominations have been losing members since the 1970s. Many continue to decline in membership. For example, the Presbyterian Church (U.S.A.) has lost 30 percent of its membership since 1960.[2]

The reasons for membership decline are complex. Other authors have dealt with them exhaustively. They include demographic factors and other causes outside the congregation. Here we look only at those causes within the control of the local church. Considerable evidence supports the conclusion that member dropouts are a major cause of mainline membership decline.

Concerned congregations may focus on member recruitment on the assumption that conservative churches grow because of their ability to attract new members. However, research reveals that conservative denominations grow principally because of their ability to keep their transferring members and the children of members. It shows that membership decline in many mainline denominations results from their inability to do so.

Membership loss is of special urgency for congregations whose local context is unfavorable to church growth. If they are to survive, they must keep members they already have, rather than depend on attracting new ones.

Why another book on congregational vitality and retention of members? Some authors have dealt extensively with the assimilation of new members. They tell us we must involve them in small groups, in specific tasks, or in places of leadership in the congregation. Others have written on congregational vitality and church growth. There are excellent programs that reclaim inactive members. They train lay pastors to hear members' cries of pain and to minister to them. Many have written on conflict management, but largely without spelling out its impact on membership retention. There are works on meeting the needs of youth and young adults (groups that most congregations are losing every day).

However, no one, to my knowledge, has brought all these things together in a brief but comprehensive summary of the issues involved. Nor have I found a guide to the many approaches that congregations can take to come alive and keep their members.

This book is the result of extensive research described in the preface. It assumes that the way to discover what bonds members to congregations is to study churches that have been successful in doing so.

One major conclusion stands out: Churches that meet members' deep needs will attract and keep them. The glue that holds them is there when members experience caring community and discover meaning for living. It is strengthened when they engage in meaningful service and feel that they really belong. There are specific things that congregations believe and are and do that make a difference.

This book then is a guide to the development of member loyalty through vibrant Christian community. First, it is a reference handbook for creative planning. It provides a clear and comprehensive outline, covering possible ways to enhance congregational vitality and strengthen its power to bond members to its life and work. Each chapter contains ideas, programs, or approaches that have proven value. This is followed by a list of other resources upon which pastors and officers may draw.

Second, this is a study book that lay leaders, pastors, and interested members may use to gain an understanding of those things that contribute to membership retention. Study questions at the end of each chapter will be useful in adult education classes, church officer retreats, seminary classrooms, or professional workshops.

Each chapter begins with a brief analysis of the issues the chapter addresses. Then comes a description of various possible courses of positive action. There are illustrations of the ways churches of different sizes in different settings have dealt with the issues. This includes options suggested by other studies.

Readers will have varied backgrounds and particular interests. Some will review the issues quickly and move immediately to actions they might take. Others will want to explore the issues in depth. They can study the section on analysis, ponder the study questions or discuss them with others, and engage in further suggested reading.

Of course, each congregation is unique. There are significant differences between large and small membership churches. I have been particularly careful to include many illustrations from small churches. They are a majority in any denomination.

The usefulness of this book will depend upon imaginative adaptation of its many options. Not every suggestion will be helpful to every congregation. Each pastor and board will need to select approaches that fit their unique situation.

A good cook collects many recipes. Each might appeal to different palates under the right circumstances. Some may never prove to be useful. All hone a cook's skill in combining ingredients to fit daily fare or festive celebration. In planning a menu, the chef considers the purpose of the occasion and the guests who will enjoy the meal. After selecting the most appropriate dishes, good cooks will probably adapt the recipe to their own styles of cooking.

Some approaches may be appropriate in a very large church and some in a very small church. Some will be effective in small towns and others in large cities. The book tries to point out some of these differences. However, pastors, church officers, or boards, like skilled chefs, will need to choose those that will be useful in their congregations. Some may prove to be irrelevant. Hopefully at least a few will provide the special spark that will light a new fire in your church.

RESOURCES

Hoge, Dean R., and David A. Roozen. *Understanding Church Growth and Decline: 1950–1978.* New York and Philadelphia: The Pilgrim Press, 1979.

Smith, Donald P. "Closing the Back Door." In *The Mainstream Protestant "Decline": The Presbyterian Pattern,* edited by Milton J Coalter, John M. Mulder, and Louis B. Weeks, 86–101. Louisville, Ky.: Westminster/John Knox Press, 1990. This essay contains extensive notes that document many statements made in the present book.

1

OPEN YOUR WINDOWS

A vital congregation draws its members inward like a magnet. That vitality also attracts visitors, draws them into its fellowship, and results in evangelism.

When the new pastor arrived, Plainfield Church was surviving tenaciously with a maintenance mentality. Its sixty-five aging members had grown up together in the farming town of forty-five hundred. The pastor's call included a yoked congregation nearly thirty miles away. The people had to be content with a part-time pastor, but they were used to doing for themselves.

Eight years later, many of the same people are there, but others have joined them. The church has grown to more than a hundred, and Sunday worship attendance is equal to about two-thirds of its membership. More important, there is a vibrant, upbeat quality about their life together. What has happened in the intervening years?

A demographer would point to the development of a new housing area about five miles out of town. It serves as a bedroom community for a good-sized city not far away. That has helped provide the potential for numerical growth. But what of growth in spirit? Most members would point to the pastor as the source of new energy and creativity. The pastor, in turn, would credit members who are open to growth. The other congregation, he explains, has not been so open. However, this congregation has been a fertile seed bed in which vigorous Christian lives can grow.

All these things have made their contribution. But listen to what the pastor says:*

Three years ago God's Spirit started working in some of our members and in me. I had been going to small-church seminars and had learned many of the advantages of a small church. "Be happy you are small," they told us. Then an evangelism conference changed the way I inter-

---

*Unless attributed otherwise, quoted material throughout this volume is taken from interviews with pastors and church members or from their responses to the author's questionnaires.

preted scripture and prayer. Suddenly I realized there are a lot of unchurched people out there. I shifted from a survival mentality to an outreach outlook.

Within six months a lot of things began to happen. Spontaneously, two of our women started looking out for visitors. They would follow up on the telephone or visit them. A young lady transferred her membership from another congregation where she had been dissatisfied. She became a spark plug for many things. She started a second adult Sunday school class and the session blessed it. Then there was a second women's group at a more convenient time for working women. Most of our programs grew out of responsiveness to need and to growth. One hundred percent of new members came by invitation. People felt accepted immediately. It was amazing! God's Spirit was at work and we basked in it.

Probing deeper, we discover that members find meaning for life in their Bible study and in the pastor's sermons. "Every week," one says, "he gives us something that helps us deal with our everyday experiences as Christians. People even talk about the sermon in Monday morning car pools."

The pastor finds his satisfaction in preaching, administering the sacraments, and helping people exercise their God-given gifts. "If someone wants to do something," he says, "we say, 'Okay, go ahead.' Then I support them in what they are doing and channel to them the additional resources they need to be successful."

He is a good organizer and provides patient, low-key, but forceful leadership. He helps the congregation set goals for its work. In small dinner groups of eight he has engaged members in study of what the church should be about and shared various options with participants. They channel suggestions back to the session. "Ideas need time to percolate," he points out. "Then someone will bring it up and the session will act."

Out of such study, the need for more work with families became clear. Jointly with the community education program, the church sponsored an Active Parenting class. This served both members of the church and parents from the community at large.

This caring congregation draws its members more deeply into its life because it meets their needs for fellowship and meaning. Yet this is not a self-centered congregation. Within the parish area, about half the population is Hispanic or African American, and there is a section of low-income housing. Two out of five school children are in the free lunch program. A member of the church is tutoring one young adult in reading.

"If our members see a need," the pastor says, "they'll find a way to get the money." One recent Christmas they became aware of a divorced single mother with two children who was in desperate need. They gave her $250. At the time, they did not realize that this prevented her from being evicted from her home. In her childhood, several step-fathers had sexually abused her. For over a year the church, at its expense, sent her to the nearby city for counseling.

What is congregational vitality? It is the Holy Spirit at work in the lives of pastors, church officers, and members. It is the love of God moving members beyond the limitations of natural human friendships. It is a Christ-centered company of wounded healers. Operationally, we recognize it when a large proportion of a congregation's members are

actively participating in its worship, study, fellowship, and planning,

continuously growing in their understanding of the Christian faith and deepening their commitment to Jesus Christ,

consistently incorporating others into full participation in the life, leadership, and decision making of the church,

quietly caring for each other and serving in the community,

vigorously involved in concern for justice and compassion in the world.

Nicodemus said it for us. "How can these things be?" The wind blows where it chooses. We hear the sound of it and feel its power but do not really know where it comes from or where it goes.

For many years now, I have had on the wall of my office, and now of my bedroom, a drab picture by Andrew Wyeth. From a humble, colorless room with a crack in the wall, one looks out on a dreary countryside. A little dirt road leads to the world beyond. The crinkled old window shades reveal our very ordinary circumstances. On a sultry day, a fresh wind is blowing the aged lace curtains back into our room.

Here is a parable of our lives as individuals and as churches. The winds of God are always blowing. We do not generate the wind, but we need it desperately if we are to live. We are not simply passive recipients of grace. God calls us to do our part. We must respond by opening the windows of our souls and of our churches. Our lives or our congregation may seem hopeless. Our part is to look around and find windows that we can open to the Spirit of God.

When Jesus says, "You must be born from above," he calls us to take responsibility for the birth of vitality. We are to be ready for God's winds of change and to prepare ourselves to receive them.

This book is about congregational vitality and its power to bond members to a particular church. We shall examine in some detail the elements that generate such vitality and give many examples of what congregations have done to foster it.

We shall see that congregations can develop member loyalty when they meet diverse needs, cultivate caring communities, communicate meaning for living, serve others, shape society, and incorporate members diligently. We shall examine ways that bonding churches equip and enable lay shepherds, channel conflicts creatively, nourish families and support singles, empower youth, span the young adult years, and enrich the lives of seniors. We shall discover how pastors may lead vigorously as servants.

QUESTIONS FOR STUDY AND DISCUSSION

1. Do you agree with the definition of congregational vitality in this chapter? If not, how would *you* define it?

2. In what ways does your church meet the definition of congregational vitality? In what ways are you different?

3. Decide on one or two of the most important ways your congregation might change in order to be a more vital church. What could your members do to open windows to the winds of the Spirit?

2

MEET DIVERSE NEEDS

Bonding churches meet the different needs of their members. Some do it naturally, others purposefully. As one pastor put it, "If the church does not meet the spiritual, social, psychological, and physical needs of the people, it will not grow. We aim to have a comprehensive ministry. We say, find a hurt and heal it. Discover a need and meet it."

The needs of people vary. Even in outwardly homogeneous congregations, individuals are unique in personality, age, marital status, and family composition. They vary in education, interests, occupation, and life-style. Their perceived needs, commitments, and stages of faith development are different. Bonding churches are aware of this and plan accordingly.

Ten years ago Ocean View Church had five hundred members. It had been through a bruising conflict. An excellent interim minister had brought healing to the people, and they had called a new pastor. Today they have fifteen hundred members and an average Sunday worship attendance of fourteen hundred in a sanctuary that seats eight hundred. What has happened in the meantime?

When Dr. Black arrived, he decided that breadth would be the goal of his ministry. His session and his staff now share that commitment. Broad program offerings appeal to different interests and concerns. "We take people seriously," they say. "We are sensitive to their needs. We spend a lot of time listening. Expressed needs can open the door to meeting deeper needs of which people are unaware."

There are three services on Sunday morning. The eight o'clock contemporary service is popular with younger folk. Young men and women, dressed informally, lead with guitar and popular religious songs. A member offers prayer, responding to requests from the congregation. The preacher wears business attire. At 9:30 there is a traditional Reformed service with choir robes, pulpit gowns, formal prayers, and familiar hymns. The sanctuary fills with young parents and their children, youth, and senior adults. The eleven o'clock traditional service always includes communion. The sermon at each service is identical.

Some congregations unnecessarily avoid different services for fear that they might be divisive. Church officers and staff in this congregation find their unity in commitment to biblical preaching and teaching and in a Christ-centered ministry. Beyond that, however, they welcome many theological perspectives, with freedom for liberal and conservative points of view. There is a small group of charismatics in the church.

ETHNIC DIVERSITY IN SUBURBIA

Recently, Ocean View Church made a bold bid in the direction of ethnic diversity. The church is located in an affluent neighborhood close to the border of Mexico. An influx of Mexican migrants has caused considerable community tension. For more than a year the church has employed a part-time Hispanic parish associate. Under his leadership, about a hundred worshipers gather each Sunday for a Spanish-language service.

Rather than trying to develop a separate congregation at this time, the session decided to integrate the Hispanic worshipers into its own membership. Out of the first group of twenty who united with the church, five were baptized. With financial assistance from larger judicatories, a full-time Hispanic pastor is to be added to the staff. The pastor's vision of diversity has grown beyond theological, programmatic, and liturgical inclusiveness. It now challenges the responsive congregation to take community leadership in demonstrating the unity of all cultures as part of the family of God.

It is their hope that enough Hispanic members will share in the fellowship ultimately to make possible the spin-off of a self-supporting Spanish-speaking congregation. Toward that end, Ocean View Church has committed itself to a large financial investment in that future.

PROGRAMS CAN MEET DIFFERING NEEDS

"Something for everyone" is a common theme in bonding churches of all sizes. "The more things serve people, the more bonding there will be," they say. "Members come with their own agendas. We address those needs right where they live. This has led us into several new program areas. A variety of social, educational, and spiritual opportunities is essential."

Most churches can no longer depend on heritage ties to serve as membership glue. There is too much mobility in our population. For most members, loyalty to the congregation depends on the extent to which they can affirm its goals and participate in its programs.[1]

What programs are most likely to call forth such a positive response? Of course, this varies with each congregation's particular constituencies. In general, however, we identified a number of specific programs that bonding churches are more likely to offer than are high-loss churches. More than 60 percent had Sunday schools for children, Bible study groups, youth groups, and children's choirs. More than half had young adult programs, prayer groups, and member visitation. More than 30 percent sponsored an overseas missionary; offered marriage, family, and parenting classes; and had youth choirs. Roughly one-fourth of the churches offered singles programs and opportunities to study social justice issues or to develop global awareness.

LARGE CHURCHES

Large-membership churches can offer a wide array of programs. This is one of their strengths, and they must capitalize on it. We found that members of large bonding churches are more likely than members of large high-loss churches to be satisfied with the number and variety of programs available to them. Such satisfaction is particularly strong in high-attendance churches of more than two hundred members.

One conclusion of the *Effective Christian Education* study tempers our finding. It suggests that "effective Christian education can be transmitted through a small number of programs and events, as long as, in combination, they have effective leadership, process, and content. Accordingly, what matters is how things are done rather than numbers or range of programs. This finding should be especially encouraging to the small congregation."[2]

SMALL CHURCHES

Very small churches do not have the resources to offer a long menu of programs. However, they can concentrate on a few select activities that respond to the concerns of most of their people. They can also satisfy individual yearnings through personal contact with members rather than through programs.

Small churches are usually oriented to relationships rather than to programs. Friendships glue them together. Nevertheless, our study found that small bonding churches are more likely than small high-loss churches to have Sunday schools for children, youth groups, young adult programs, and programs in marriage, family, and parenting. As chapter 9 makes clear, these attract and keep families in the church. Small bonding churches are also more likely to have church officer training and member visitation programs. More of them sponsor an overseas missionary and seek to develop international or global awareness.

THREE TROUBLING QUESTIONS

Before proceeding further, we must answer three questions that may trouble some readers:

1. Is it legitimate to focus on meeting members' needs if a congregation wants to be faithful to the gospel?

2. Does a commitment to diversity really attract and keep church members?

3. Will an emphasis on meeting different needs lead to division in a congregation?

First, are we faithful to the gospel if we focus on meeting people's needs? Should we not serve God rather than people? Are we not pandering to members if we aim to please them? Is not faithfulness to the gospel the only criteria for congregational life?

Our answer is quick and clear. Faithfulness to the gospel requires that we meet people's needs. Jesus was always responsive to the needs of people around him. He heard their cries of pain and responded by healing, teaching, forgiving, and empowering.

Jesus was also aware that people do not always know why they feel empty. He knew that all of us lack peace until we are reconciled to God and to each other. He knew that life is empty until we reach out in self-giving. So he acted to deal with hidden shortcomings as well as with longings that people expressed. In fact he had a matchless ability to distinguish one from the other. Jesus did not hesitate to condemn the religious leaders of his day. He was not just a crowd pleaser. Judgment and reconciliation are part of meeting our real needs.

For the church to equivocate on the importance of meeting human need is to abdicate the gospel. "Our goal," said one pastor, "is to meet all people at their place of need in the name of Jesus."

Second, does a focus on diversity attract and bond members, or does it inhibit the growth and effectiveness of a congregation? The Institute on Church Growth advocates homogeneity. When there are several differing constituencies in the community, it tells us to concentrate on one of them while remaining open to others. Its research shows that churches grow when they seek and retain "our kind of people."

In contrast to this, we are convinced that the ability of a mainline congregation to deal creatively with diversity makes an important contribution to attracting and retaining church members. Mainline parishes tend to be more heterogeneous than other voluntary organizations. If they do not meet the needs of their multiple constituencies, participation declines and they lose members. David S. Steward articulates the mainline conviction when he says, "The church exists to help us value and interpret our differences within God's world, rather than to divide us according to social prejudices."[3] Our study tends to confirm Steward's claim that dropouts are waiting for the church to live out the gospel as a diverse community with many gifts.

Third, does an emphasis on diversity lead to division? Diversity can divide if not properly channeled. However, it also can have a healthy, stimulating, and bonding effect. This requires affirmation of diversity and cultivation of a strong unifying force. We found that congregations that manage differences effectively have preaching and teaching that is biblically based and Christ-centered. They give their members active and effective pastoral care. Their small groups encourage dialogue on volatile issues within a climate of fairness and respect for those with differing views.

A church of six hundred members in the Southeast with an average autumn worship attendance of 350 has many different kinds of people among its members. Socio-economically, they range from millionaires to unemployed young couples in mixed marriages. Many are middle-class managers and administrators or professionals. Theologically, there are "new evangelicals, old liberals, and medium Presbyterians," to use the pastor's description. On the explosive issue of abortion, the membership includes both pro-choice and right-to-life advocates.

How do they handle their differences? Expository sermons interpret such great biblical themes as the nature of God, Christ, and the Holy Spirit. They help worshipers face common experiences of tragedy, suffering, and loneliness. "In our worship," the pastor explains, "we seek to deal with people's spiritual heartaches."

Application of the gospel to social issues is done in classes and committees where dialogue can take place. There they insist on a fair process, on carefully listening to points of view other than one's own, and on learning from one another. They encourage disagreement. "Our unity is in Christ," explains the pastor. "We can disagree about other things. We keep a good focus on the major beliefs of the Christian church and emphasize that there are many authentic ways of serving our Lord. In committee decisions, we are a democracy under the Lordship of Christ."

Active pastoral care also helps this congregation avoid destructive conflict. Pastors and lay leaders work together to discover and minister to the pain of their people. The pastors spend a great deal of time interacting with members and praying with them. They do much hospital calling and counseling. When members feel that people really care, they are less likely to embroil themselves in combat with the pastor or with others in the congregation.

This style of ministry has much to commend it. If people are spiritually hungry and torn by inner conflicts, they cannot cope with the world around them. If their souls are malnourished, their passion for social action will soon wither away.

However, there is also a danger in this approach. If preaching and teaching focus only on personal and family needs, members may miss the prophetic demands of the biblical story. They may not be able to apply their faith to complex ethical issues in our society. And members who have a sensitive social conscience and a passion for social justice may drift away because they feel the church is irrelevant.

I am convinced that many pastors could be more forthright in interpreting social issues than they think, if they would do so from a biblical perspective that members can understand and if they have first won the right to be heard by demonstrating a caring heart. Chapter 5 will develop this idea further.

POSITIVE APPROACHES TO INDIVIDUAL DIFFERENCES

Instinctively people look upon disagreements as problems. The transforming approach is to understand them as opportunities. This is what Paul does in 1 Corinthians 12. When he wants the Christians in Corinth to settle their conflicts, he uses the image of a unified body with many differing parts.

Leaders can learn to respond positively to the rich diversity they encounter in their congregations. The first step is to understand some of the important ways in which individuals differ. This can help them be more responsive in their ministries to individuals. It can transform administrative tension into cooperative endeavor. We deal here with three positive approaches to such understanding.

PEOPLE ARE DIFFERENT IN THEIR PERSONALITIES

The Myers-Briggs Type Indicator,* which is based in Jungian psychology, has become increasingly popular among church leaders. It is a powerful tool for understanding the way in which individual preferences can complement one another rather than create problems in our interpersonal relationships.

---

*Myers-Briggs Type Indicator® is a registered trademark of Consulting Psychologists Press, Inc.

Studies have found that people tend to prefer different styles of understanding the world about them and of deciding how to act in it. These preferences are neither bad nor good. In combination they describe people with distinctive interests and abilities who often make diverse occupational choices.

People with opposite types of style preference are likely to have opposite strengths and weaknesses. They may find it difficult to understand each other and may experience strained relationships or conflict. However, when people understand their different style preferences, they can complement one another and enjoy creative and productive relationships. Use of the Myers-Briggs Type Indicator can help develop such understanding.

Knowledge of type preferences has positive potential for enhanced ministry when pastors recognize and use their strengths and when they supplement their weaknesses by encouraging others to use complementary strengths. One pastor puts it this way:

> Most of the business people in my congregation are the opposite of me in almost every category. Rather than seeing them as "the enemy," I have asked a group of them to help me with personnel decisions and the administration of the church, and they have done a tremendous job. They have abilities that complement mine. The chairman of the worship committee, our music director, and I deliberately seek out different personality types to give us feedback on sermons, music, and the order of worship.[4]

This pastor knows that most church officers are like 75 percent of the population. They prefer to understand situations by using their senses to get the facts. They need this in business and finance. On the other hand, most pastors use intuition as their favorite approach. This is consistent with their interest in understanding life from a theological perspective. These different styles can lead to misunderstandings and conflicts.

When people understand each other, they can develop a complementary working relationship. Intuitive pastors need sensing laity to clarify what it will take to carry out their vision. And factually oriented church officers can profit from the vision that pastors bring. Pastors who recognize how many factually oriented people there are in their congregations can enhance their preaching and teaching by using very concrete illustrations that give flesh and blood to abstract truth.

Some people prefer to delay decisions as long as possible while they explore different options and gather additional information. Others are uncomfortable when things are left up in the air. They want to make plans and reach decisions. Two strong members with opposite styles can immobilize a committee. Pastors who prefer to delay making decisions can frustrate associate pastors who prefer to make careful plans. Their style can exasperate church officers who are oriented toward making decisions. An understanding of their different style preferences can help all concerned to make necessary accommodations in working together.

People Differ in Their Stage of Faith Development

In his videotaped lecture, *Why Active Members Stay Active,* John S. Savage draws on findings from a major research project by Kenneth Stokes involving interviews with thirty thousand people from a hundred denominations.[5] The six stages listed by Savage provide a helpful framework for understanding the faith needs of parishioners at critical transition points in their lives. Ages given are approximate and will vary from individual to individual.

The age of differentiation (eighteen to twenty-five years of age). The three primary tasks are finding a mate (or postponing it for a career), finding an occupation, and developing a value system. The primary religious question is Am I a spiritual clone or do I have a faith of my own? Because many dropouts occur during this life stage, we shall look at it more carefully in chapter 11 on young adult ministries.

The years of boredom (thirty to thirty-two years of age). Life has become routine for those who have established their life patterns. The faith questions are Is this all there is? What is the real meaning of life? Why are we really here?

The recapitulation years, the mid-life crisis (thirty-eight to forty-one years of age). Awareness of one's inevitable death comes to the fore as peers begin to die. Skills that have been effective in earlier life don't work any more. Issues not dealt with at any of the prior stages are reworked. This may lead one to take a new mate, new career, new philosophy or theology.

The years of the empty nest (fifty to fifty-five years of age). The fact that life is transitory is now real. The questions are What can I do for which I will be remembered? What can I do that will be meaningful, productive, and helpful to others? If other stages have been successfully traversed, faith begins to mellow.

The years of letting go (sixty to sixty-five years of age). Employment ends for many. For some, this can mean a loss of identity. Others reinvest in different meaningful activities.

THE YEARS OF APPROACHING DEATH (seventy and over). People lose their spouses and sell their homes. Deprivation from such losses can be traumatic.

One who has successfully negotiated the earlier transitions can be a gentle, warm adult Christian who is characterized by acceptance, serenity, wisdom, compassion, and openness. However, one who has failed to deal with those transitions can become bitter, brittle, critical, and frightened.

Savage points out that a cluster of events at any one of the major life transitions may lead members to drop out. At each critical transition, one must find supportive friends and support groups to keep going.

PEOPLE DIFFER IN THE PROGRAM EMPHASES THEY SEEK

Among United Methodist churches, Warren J. Hartman of the denomination's General Board of Discipleship identified five different audiences. They focus on fellowship, evangelism, study of the faith, social ministries, or a combination of two or more of these concerns. He found that members in each group are different in their personal characteristics, their theology, their expectations of church and church school, and their participation patterns.[6]

Our study found no differences in the proportion of members in bonding or high-loss churches that favored one or another of these options. Most members in more than half the congregations favor a combination of more than one emphasis. A majority in almost half the congregations favor a principal emphasis on fellowship. Significant minorities favor one or another of the other program areas. All this affirms the value of diverse program offerings. It also suggests the importance of keeping a programmatic balance that will enable people to meet their differing goals without competition or conflict.

Working with marvelously different parishioners can be like weaving a beautiful tapestry. The artisan who creates the picture must understand the different colored threads and how they contrast or blend on the loom. Assorted hues and distinctive materials of varied weight and texture come together in a harmonious whole.

The challenge is great because this is a living picture. It is continually expanding and contracting. The reflection of its lights and shadows come and go. Those who weave need to know how quickly change takes place. Threads can get snarled in conflict or snagged and broken. They can dissolve or completely disappear from the picture. One day there is beautiful variety; the next a horrible knotted tangle.

You the pastor, church officer, or other leader are part of the tapestry. You also join the Holy Spirit as co-artists who create the living tapestry by what you do or fail to do. How then can one discover the needs and expectations that people bring to their life in the congregation? And what principles can guide a congregation in dealing with its diversity?

PRINCIPLES FOR DEALING WITH DIVERSITY

1. Look upon differences as an asset rather than a liability.

2. Set your goal for breadth of ministry. Plan for it. Creative diversity must be persistently intentional.

3. Recognize, identify, and affirm the differences in your community, in your constituency, and in your congregation. Legitimize them in your preaching and teaching.

4. Clearly articulate the unity that binds your diversity together. The larger or more diverse the congregation, the more important this is. It comes largely through services of worship and preaching the Word.

5. Discover and keep in tune with the needs of your constituencies by such methods as
    a. Getting to know them through pastoral visitation and other informal contacts.
    b. Asking new members about their expectations.
    c. Asking members through pew cards or questionnaires.
    d. Evaluating programs by discussion with participants or by written instruments.
    e. Getting reports from deacons and other callers in members' homes.
    f. Holding home meetings with members to discuss what programs are most important to them.
    g. Including representatives from different organizations or groups in your planning processes.
    h. Discussing members' unmet needs in the boards of the congregation.

6. Love your membership into acceptance of differences through consistent pastoral care.

7. Organize for diversity. Small groups are natural arenas for the expression of different perspectives. Encourage them to take initiatives and give them freedom to do so.

8. Lead gently, gradually, persistently. Generate opportunities for personal interaction and fellowship with diverse people. This can come when very different people work together.

In this chapter we have been looking at the importance of recognizing and meeting the *differing* needs of parishioners. In the next four chapters we describe four needs that are *common* to all people. Our study found bonding churches were more effective than high-loss churches in meeting their members' needs for an accepting and caring fellowship, ultimate meaning for living, involvement in significant service to others, and belonging to a supportive community. We shall now examine the ways in which each of these four needs bonds members to the congregation.

QUESTIONS FOR STUDY AND DISCUSSION

1. In what ways is your congregation diverse? What proportion of your members are elderly? Middle-aged? Young adults? Young people? Single? Married without children? Married with children? Single parents? Etc.

2. How do you discover the needs of members in your congregation? In the community that you serve? Do you do this consciously? If so, how often?

3. What are the most important needs of members in your congregation? How well do your present programs meet them?

4. What other approaches might your congregation use to meet the needs of your constituencies more effectively than you now do?

5. In your congregation, what possibilities do you see for using the Myers-Briggs Type Indicator? The stages of faith development? The five audiences for different program emphases?

RESOURCES

Kiersey, David, and Marilyn Bates. *Please Understand Me: Character and Temperament Types.* Del Mar, Calif.: Prometheus Nemesis Books, 1978.

Kliewer, Stephen. *How to Live with Diversity in the Local Church.* Washington, D.C.: The Alban Institute, 1987.

Myers, Isabel Briggs. *Introduction to Type.* Palo Alto, Calif.: Consulting Psychologists Press, 1981.

Savage, John S. *Why Active Members Stay Active.* Reynoldsburg, Ohio: L.E.A.D. Consultants, Inc., 1987. Videotape.

3

CULTIVATE CARING
COMMUNITIES

Caring love and meaning for living are like the resin and hardener in epoxy glue. Together they cement a member's loyalty to the congregation. If either is diminished, bonding suffers. Chapter 4 discusses meaning for living. Here we examine the bonding power of caring communities.

Friendship ties are powerful bonding forces. They attract new members and deter dropouts. We found that members in bonding churches are more likely than members in high-loss churches to have many friends in the congregation. The more friends members have in a church the more actively they will participate in it. Friendships may draw a person toward two groups at the same time. If the stronger of those bonds is with the present church, a member is likely to stay there. If something breaks those bonds or weakens them, or if other important needs are not being met, the risk of leaving increases.

THE IMPORTANT ROLE OF FRIENDSHIP ACTIVITIES

The pressures of our mobile society have fragmented life for most Americans. Therefore, it is especially important for the church to enable development of significant friendships. Our culture has shifted from local community to extended family, to nuclear family "and finally to the lonely individual moving from place to place, and institution to institution, dealing with each if, and as much as, it serves his needs and interests."[1] For many, multiple moves have severed strong local ties.

Broken ties lead to dropouts. As many as half the dropouts occur when members move and fail to unite with a church in their new location. Mobile members drop out because their lives no longer revolve around a local community. They live in one neighborhood, work in another, enjoy recreation in still another, and shop somewhere else. Thus, even when the church is nearby, it is only a small piece of their lives.

Yet these same people are hungry for meaningful relationships. When they find them in a congregation, they are drawn inexorably into its deeper Christian fellowship.

THE COHESIVE POWER OF CHRISTIAN COMMUNITY

But people need more than friendship. In bonding churches members forge friendships within the context of a caring Christian community. Together members enjoy fellowship activities and join in a search for meaning within a common commitment to Christ. In the company of fellow pilgrims, they study, pray, and reach out in service.

Our study found that members in bonding churches are more likely than members in high-loss churches to feel that they belong, are accepted, loved, and supported. They are more likely to say that the congregation provides them with a warm network of supporting relationships. For them, the congregation is like a warm, caring family. Members of high attendance churches also are more likely to have these feelings.

A warm, caring Christian community is one of the first things visitors notice and one of the last things members relinquish. The *Effective Christian Education* study found that such a community contributes to faith development and to congregational loyalty.

BEHOLD HOW THEY LOVE ONE ANOTHER

Vibrant with caring love and buzzing with activity, Crossroads Church sits in the middle of a corn field in the heart of the Midwest. On a typical fall Sunday up to two-thirds of its 150 members gather for worship. The cohesive power of Christian community is evident to any visitor who experiences their welcome.

"These are wonderful people," the pastor exclaims with excitement and admiration in her voice. "They enjoy each other's company, and no one feels a stranger here. The church means a lot to them, both young and old."

"Each year we have a super-duper, whiz-bang service to honor the choir, the confirmation class, or some other group. It brings out the whole congregation."

When they honored members over sixty-five years of age, everyone got involved. Young couples drove the honorees to church. Young people met them, opened the car doors, and escorted them into the church. While video cameras whirred, each honoree received a corsage or boutonniere. Children served punch and cookies prepared by women of the church. During the service the pastor read the name of each honored member from the printed bulletin. Each received a certificate of appreciation prepared by a congregational calligrapher.

This church has picnics, breakfasts, and suppers. A fellowship group for adults of all ages enjoys square dancing, volleyball, and softball. In a "road rally," their cars zig-zag over the area to an unknown goal. They find their way by answering ten questions, many of them from the Bible. At each intersection, if their answer to the next question is yes, they turn to the right; if no, they turn left. Finally, when they admit they are lost, a "Help!" envelope reveals their destination. In the end, all arrive and the party begins.

Each year, on four Sundays in June, the young people erect a platform in front of the church and conduct a half-hour evening vesper service. People participate from their cars parked on the lawn or bring their lawn chairs. On one of the Sundays they then enjoy an ice cream social.

Members are caring people. One family could not afford the clothes their daughter needed for eighth-grade graduation. The pastor took the girl shopping for a complete outfit including shoes, jewelry, and a hair bow. An anonymous member paid for it.

A mother in the community was jailed for drunken driving. Members of the congregation rallied to help her children during her absence. And when she returned, without a license, they visited her each week and took her shopping.

"There is a spirit in this church," the pastor concludes, "and you can feel it. I can't explain it, but you know it. There's a lot of love here."

WHERE FRIENDSHIP TIES COME NATURALLY

As many have observed, friendship ties are characteristic of small churches. Bonding churches accentuate this. Almost all members in 58 percent of small bonding churches have many friends in the congregation compared with only 35 percent of small high-loss churches.

Some small churches in small stable communities told us that member retention is not a problem. Family ties, friendships, and cultural expectations tend to keep members involved in the church. One pastor wrote:

Sixty-five percent of our family units are related to one family. Except for a handful of recent arrivals, members have known each other virtually all their lives. Therefore, there is an internal pressure on members to remain active in the congregation. From time to time a family will move to another church in the area due to feelings which have built up over a long period. Occasionally, they return to our congregation after a cooling-off period. Such movement away, however, is pretty rare.

We make a special effort to include representatives of all families and branches in special activities, such as when four families lead the lighting of the Advent candles. However, this is in the interest of fairness and peace, not specifically to retain members. Loyalty to the family and to the church keep us going. It would take a real fight to move most of the congregation away.

Such congregations might aim

to help their members find ultimate meaning in life,

to exercise consistent and loving pastoral care,

to cultivate sensitivity to the ways in which family ties and close friendships keep new members from being accepted,

to enhance natural friendship ties by activities designed to incorporate new members into the fellowship circle,

to meet varied individual needs by providing as many options as possible within the congregation's limited resources,

to avoid destructive conflict by adequate communication and involving members in decision making,

to encourage acceptance of new members in committee assignments or offices.

FELLOWSHIP ACTIVITIES

One large bonding church uses a fellowship committee composed of a representative of each group in the church. The committee coordinates fellowship activities and plans churchwide programs. Representatives then promote those programs in their groups.

Such a group could

review all the opportunities for fellowship offered by the congregation and its organizations;

discover for each activity the participation level of youth, young adults, couples, families, singles, seniors, or others;

ask representatives of those segments what fellowship needs are not being met; and

initiate additional fellowship opportunities to meet them.

As stimulus to such a process, we offer a summary of fellowship activities found in the bonding churches.

CONGREGATIONWIDE ACTIVITIES

RETREATS. A get-away weekend for the whole congregation once or twice a year offers family fun, recreation, study, and worship. Crafts, music, story time, movies, etc., for children are led by college students who are paid a nominal amount. There are youth activities, adult mixers, intergenerational games, worship, singing, a campfire, or a talent show. A visiting speaker and adult Bible study provides inspiration. Communion on Sunday morning closes the time together. Members return with new or deeper friendships and with excitement for the new church year.

New members are especially invited. Success of such a retreat will depend upon setting up committees to plan different parts of the program well in advance. Also the pastor needs to promote it enthusiastically.

EATING TOGETHER. Activities could include the following:

Dinners or breakfasts celebrating special seasons (e.g., Advent, Christmas, Lent, Easter, Mother's Day, Thanksgiving).

Recognition dinners for members with fifty or more years of continuous membership. Issue special invitations and request a reply. Put names in the bulletin and in a newspaper article.

Dinners in someone's home to honor new members.

Recognition dinners for graduating seniors, choir members, or any other group.

Annual work nights at the church with a catered dinner.

Monthly potlucks with speakers or other programs.

OTHER INTERGENERATIONAL POSSIBILITIES include:

A pie-sing: Members nominate their favorite hymns in advance. A congregational sing gives hymn backgrounds and members tell why they chose the hymn. Pie is served.

Picnics, ice cream socials, or community luncheons.

A strawberry festival with covered dishes, a magician, games, and musical entertainment.

A father-child picnic with hot-dogs, hamburgers, and munchies.

A Christmas happening to make ornaments.

SUNDAY MORNING FELLOWSHIP ACTIVITIES could involve the following:

A coffee/juice fellowship hour, which is particularly important between services when congregations start a second Sunday service.

A continental breakfast or brunch before or after service.

A potluck dinner after worship once a month.

A worship service at a park, followed by a picnic, or a picnic after regular worship.

Photographs of all members, or of new members with their names, could be posted on a bulletin board.

PROGRAMS FOR ADULTS

DINNERS FOR EIGHT. Volunteer participants, assigned in groups of eight, dine together in one of their homes. Groups include new members, those who do not know each other very well, couples, and singles who invite someone to go with them. Some churches rotate participants each time and have dinners four times a year. Others meet monthly for as long as a year.

SECRET PALS. Individuals or families are paired together at random from a list of volunteers. Each is assigned a pal whose identity they know. Each is also assigned as a pal to someone else whose name they do not know. They try to learn as much as they can about their known pals, send cards or flowers, or do other nice things for them. At the end of the year there is a "revealing party" where people learn the identity of their secret pal.

WORKING TEAMS. Members are assigned various tasks in rotation so people who do not know each other will work together. A special effort is made to include newcomers.

FELLOWSHIP WITHIN ORGANIZATIONS

Church school classes, women's circles, choirs, and other groups can foster fellowship naturally. In several churches we found an excellent example in their "Mariners" program.

Repeatedly, members of Covenant Church say that their Mariners program is the strongest force that bonds them to the church. Out of seven hundred members, 250 participate in one of the twelve "ships" in their fleet. The largest ship has fifteen couples and meets in the church. Most ships are smaller and meet in members' homes.

The national Mariners program was originally designed for couples. It seeks "to offer Christian service and outreach, to establish Christian homes, [and] to provide Christian fellowship."[2] The increased number of divorced persons, widows, and widowers has opened Mariners programs to singles as well.

At monthly meetings of each ship, volunteer hosts plan activities. Typically about half are social activities such as dinner, bowling, or a Thanksgiving dinner. Half involve discussions, Bible study, or an occasional speaker. It may be a physician who has volunteered for worldwide disaster relief or an expert on white-collar crime. Ships with parents include their children in some activities. They may have a picnic, go roller skating, or enjoy summer camping. The parents in one ship have thirty-six children who are in their early teens. They have had programs on drugs, alcohol, and child psychology.

Every ship carries some *cargo*: a work project for the church such as painting a classroom or making property repairs.

Fleet admirals and ship skippers constitute the Skippers' Council. It meets quarterly to coordinate fleet-wide service projects. During an assigned month each ship provides the Friday evening meal for 150 people in a homeless shelter. Shipmates finance, prepare, and serve the meal, and clean up afterward. Then they often go out for pizza. On different months, ships provide coffee at the Sunday morning fellowship hour.

Each year the fleet gives a Christmas party and a pre-Thanksgiving turkey dinner to benefit the church's Loaves and Fishes program. This provides meals for seniors each weekday in the fellowship hall of the church. A spring musical or talent show raises money for such projects as risers for the choir or a sound system for the sanctuary.

New members are invited to join a Mariners ship composed of others who have common interests and are within the same age range. About every two years a new ship is formed to accommodate compatible members not already in a Mariners group. Several members of an existing ship take the lead.

BEYOND FRIENDSHIP TO ACTIVE CARING

If strong bonding is to take place, relationships must move beyond friendship to active caring. Friendliness can be superficial and even self-centered if one has not learned to care for others. Members of bonding churches testify to their caring experiences.

Our son died of AIDS. The church was very supportive of him and of us. They didn't shy away from him. People hugged him. They had two Sunday classes on AIDS to help people understand. People prayed for us and for Bill. Throughout the long months our pastor was there for us. He kept close contact with us. He would seek us out on Sunday morning, and he called on the phone. He ministered to Bill's guilt. When Bill was dying, our pastor was there in minutes. So much has been done for me, I feel compelled to care about others. And when I do, it feels so good that I get positive reinforcement for my caring.

_____

After my divorce, I felt like I had one foot in the church and one foot out. I would come to Sunday worship at the last minute and slip out as quickly as possible. I didn't want to talk to anybody. I could easily have gone to another church. But people called me and said, "Peggy, this is your family. We want you here."

_____

When my husband came down with polio, I called the pastor. People called me and offered to help. They took our children to camp. The women's association furnished meals every Tuesday night for a year. And for twenty-two years two men from the church would lift Peter and his wheelchair into a car and bring him to church.

_____

People go to other churches for what they get out of it. Here they are overwhelmed by love and nurturing. They come to care for one another as a family.

HOW TO BECOME A CARING CHURCH

Repeatedly we asked members and pastors how their church had become a caring community. Reflecting on their answers, we offer the following suggestions.

START WHERE YOU ARE. Promptly identify the crisis events in people's lives.

MAKE CERTAIN THAT MEMBERS KNOW when these occur. Use the church newsletter, Sunday bulletins, or telephone chains. A prayer list in the bulletin helps. Ask for concerns and celebrations before the worship service. Then remember folks by name during the pastoral prayer. In large congregations, ushers can collect prayer request cards before the pastoral prayer.

DISCOVER CARING PERSONS and centers of caring. Give them encouragement and training. Keep them informed of needs.

PERSONALIZE CHURCH COMMUNICATIONS. List birthdays and anniversaries in the church newsletter, in the Sunday bulletin, or on the church bulletin board. In bulletins name a prayer family or an individual of the week, giving priority to new members. Continually find ways to affirm members personally and publicly.

REINFORCE CARING WHEREVER YOU FIND IT. Openly affirm specific instances of caring. The pulpit, the church newsletter, and Sunday bulletins are ideal media.

ORGANIZE FOR CARING in ways that are appropriate to your particular congregation. It is not enough for the pastor to demonstrate caring. Pastors need to mobilize the caring of the people. In small churches this may be through direct response of individuals. Larger congregations will need to develop a caring structure. Deacons normally are assigned caring functions, but do not leave caring to the deacons alone. Involve others.

MOTIVATE FOR CARING through biblical and theological preaching.

TEACH PEOPLE HOW TO CARE. Most churches in the *Effective Christian Education* study gave themselves relatively low ratings on how well members show concern and support for each other. The study concludes that education needs to emphasize the development of relational and social skills that help members know how to care.[3] People learn caring skills through such programs as Parent Effectiveness Training, Stephen Ministry, and L.E.A.D. labs. These are described in later chapters.

THE PASTOR'S ROLE

In our study key members of bonding churches were more likely than members in high-loss churches to agree strongly with two statements: "Our pastor is a warm and caring person," and "I greatly appreciate the pastoral care we receive from our minister(s)." Many see their pastors as models of caring love. "Our pastor," they say, "makes us feel wanted and important. He even remembers the names of our children."

Unfortunately, many ministers in recent years have limited their pastoral calling to serious illness, death, or other crisis situations. It is debilitating to a congregation for pastors to assume they can meet members' pastoral needs simply by being available for counseling in the church office at certain announced hours. The commitment of many bonding pastors to home visitation is impressive, even in some of the larger churches.

The pastor of a six-hundred-member church gives top priority to pastoral visitation. Every morning he is in the office. Every afternoon and evening he calls on members and their families. He is always available by beeper for crisis visitation. He visits every household at least once a year and codes his membership roll to indicate those that need more frequent visits. Some he sees every two months and some every four months according to their need. In the back of his car is a supply of books and pamphlets to meet members' differing needs. "I do the best counseling in the world in a home setting," he maintains. Once a month he meets with the witness committee and summarizes all his contacts in order for them also to get involved in calling.

Not every pastor can get involved this extensively in visitation. Chapter 7 describes lay pastoral ministries that can supplement the pastor's calling.

THE IMPACT OF A CARING STAFF

One congregation with a single pastor dramatically illustrates the value of a responsive staff. "Mary, our church secretary, is a very caring person," we heard. "She knows everyone and stays involved. In fact, she practically anticipates your needs. Her door is always open, and she ministers to everyone who walks through that door." People come in to talk with her and because she is a good listener, they soon find themselves working through their own problems.

Mary works in close teamwork with the pastor. He keeps her informed so she can reach him at any time. One morning a woman called her. "I'm pregnant," she said. "I have two children, and I can't have any more. I'm going to commit suicide." Mary left a message for the pastor and went right over to the woman's house. "I'm going to make coffee," she said. "Pastor Stevens is on his way. We'll talk." When the pastor arrived, Mary returned to the office.

CARING IS CONTAGIOUS

The best motivation for caring is to experience caring in one's own life at a time of deep need. People experience caring in their own hours of need and respond by caring for others. New members are attracted to that caring style. As they experience caring by other members, they become more caring persons themselves.

The pastor of a 230-member congregation sat with an elder and his wife until three in the morning as she was dying from a brain tumor. Years later that elder is one of their members who is most responsive to the needs of others. "He is rough and gruff," the pastor says. "He says what he thinks. But if you need him, he's there!"

A recent widow found herself with three children and without income. Close to starving, she was in desperate need. The elder helped her with rent, with food, and with getting a job. He and another elder look for opportunities to minister. Caring cultivates caring.

Perhaps Henri Nouwen says it best:

> We can only love because we are born out of love, . . . we can only give because our life is a gift, . . . we can only make others free because we are set free by Him whose heart is greater than ours. . . . We can be free to let others enter into the space created for them and allow them to dance their own dance, sing their own song and speak their own language without fear.[4]

QUESTIONS FOR STUDY AND DISCUSSION

1. What fellowship activities do you have for the whole congregation? What fellowship needs are met in your organizations? Do you meet the fellowship needs of children, youth, young adults, couples, families, singles, and seniors?

2. If you identify any unmet fellowship needs, what can you do about it? In what ways could your congregation increase its fellowship activities? Do any of the descriptions in this chapter suggest things you might do? Who might get those things to happen?

3. In what ways is your congregation a caring community? How might you improve your caring quotient? Which of the suggestions in this chapter would help motivate your members to increase their caring for each other?

RESOURCES

Presbyterian Mariners, 3704 North Belt West, Belleville, IL 62223. (618) 234-1662.

Smith, Donald P. *Congregations Alive.* Philadelphia: Westminster Press, 1981.

4

HELP MEMBERS FIND
MEANING FOR LIVING

"Do you love me? . . . Feed my sheep."

JOHN 21:17

We have seen that member loyalty depends on friendships and on participation in a caring Christian community. Now we turn to the second indispensable bonding agent. Members need to discover meaning for living through their congregational experiences.

Studies have found that people who move from one church to another or to an alternative religious movement do so in a search for meaning. They are more devout and attend church more frequently. Many have had some powerful religious experience or awakening. Those who leave churches altogether, especially young people, often have found the church meaningless. Dropouts told Gallup interviewers that a pastor or church friend who helped them deal with their doubts and find faith might attract them to the church again.

Members of bonding churches are more likely than members of high-loss churches to feel that they are being fed spiritually. They say that their pastor clearly articulates the meaning of the Christian faith for life and helps them deal with life's problems from a Christian perspective. Also, members of high-attendance churches are more likely than members of low-attendance churches to say that they discover in their congregational experiences deep meaning for their daily lives.

MEANING THROUGH PREACHING AND WORSHIP

The first place that most people look for meaning in a church is the Sunday morning worship service. They hope that the sermon will help. Bonding churches communicate meaning in their worship and in their preaching. Their services include both learning and inspiration.

A church of 265 members has an average attendance of two hundred. Its pastor speaks for others when he says, "We place a high priority on creative worship. We use lay people (young and old) as worship liturgists and acolytes. In addition, we are constantly reassessing our worship and educational offerings to assure that we are meeting members' needs."

From the perspective of the pew, we heard bonding-church members say: Worship services are meaningful and inspiring. The preaching is excellent. We understand the vocabulary. Sermons are biblically based, interesting, well-organized, and challenging. They give us something to chew on. They touch the mind, the emotions, and the will. They deal with up-to-date problems. They tie the Bible to what we are going through. Our pastor shows us how to put the gospel into practice in our lives. Our pastor feeds us; then we go into the world.

From the perspective of the pulpit, we heard bonding-church preachers say: Our worship services center in God's word. Our services speak to the concerns and challenges that come to us as individuals. The Bible is a very relevant book. I do a lot of expository preaching and connect it to people's lives based on what I know about their needs. It comes out somewhere in preaching but especially in my pastoral prayers. I am a good storyteller. When I tell Bible stories, people see themselves in the story. They say this gives them meaning for living.

Because different things are meaningful to different people, helpful preaching is not easy. One pastor's sermons speak to people where they live because he constantly visits in their homes. How else can he know what they are up against? On Sunday, he invites them to raise their questions by returning an insert in the bulletin. Unless questions are of a personal nature, he answers them later in a sermon, in a newsletter, or in announcements.

Another puts the outline of his sermon in the bulletin with blanks for members to fill out as they listen or reflect on the message. A third gives a copy of his sermon to worshipers as they arrive so they can follow what he says and discuss the message later.

MEANING THROUGH MUSIC AND DRAMA

When asked about the bonding of members to Covenant Church, the associate pastor spoke of their music program as one of the keys to their success. They have five choirs that cover all ages down to kindergarten. An adult bell choir, a children's chime choir, and a thirteen-piece orchestra play from time to time. In another bonding church we heard of the importance of drama.

As I write this, I have just come from a Sunday morning worship service in which the adult choir from another church sang Mendelssohn's *Elijah* in place of a sermon. For me and for many there, it was one of the most moving messages I have heard in a long time. The director of music, who is also the director of Christian education, prepared a folder with the words of the oratorio and a summary of Elijah's story. The crowning touch was "The Message for Today," which drew our attention to its meaning:

> Idolatry and heathenism are not merely practices of past history, for they are very much with and around us today. The ultimate question is this—Who is your God? Is it power, prestige, possessions, pleasure, money, fame, status, or . . . ? The prophet Elijah warns us of the evil of worshiping anything or anyone. For the Lord Jehovah alone is God![1]

Meaning comes to many through music, especially when the words of scripture sing themselves into our memory again and again in a favorite hymn or an oratorio. Music touches the deep stirrings of the soul.

COORDINATING PREACHING WITH ADULT EDUCATION

Bonding churches have a strong emphasis on education. Their pastors are teachers at heart and spend significant time in teaching.

Several preachers select their sermon texts from scripture passages that the adult Bible classes are studying. A church of more than four hundred members has two adult classes on Sunday mornings. The pastor teaches one on the lectionary scripture he will use that morning. The second class studies a series of issues of interest to young adults, such as "How to Be a Better Spouse." It attracts a core of young couples with attendance ranging from ten to fifteen.

The pastor of a large church told us, "I will teach at the drop of a hat! I teach the adult teachers, the Sunday school teachers, and a senior citizens group." Each Sunday several of the seven adult classes discuss the scripture on which he will base his sermon for the day. Well in advance he meets with class leaders and gives them notes on the scripture. He helps them prepare for their teaching.

That church is using the Bible Discovery curriculum. Each age group studies the same passages at their own level of understanding. So it is possible to coordinate preaching with Bible study. Because children have studied the passage, they are more likely to understand the sermon.

EFFECTIVE CHRISTIAN EDUCATION
DEVELOPS FAITH MATURITY

The *Effective Christian Education* study began with two assumptions:

1. The primary aim of congregational life is to nurture—among children, youth, and adults—a vibrant, life-changing faith, the kind of faith that shapes one's way of being, thinking, and acting.

2. A person of mature faith experiences both a life-transforming relationship to a loving God—the *vertical* theme—and a consistent devotion to serving others—the *horizontal* theme.[2]

The study found that many adults in churches do not have a well-formed faith:

For more than two-thirds of adults, faith lacks a strong vertical component, a strong horizontal component, or both. This finding presents congregations with an enormous challenge. And the challenge is even greater in their ministry to men, for whom a fully integrated faith maturity is relatively uncommon.[3]

The quality of Christian education is closely related to the development of faith maturity in youth and in adults. The study found modest relationships between faith maturity and a thinking climate, a climate of warmth, quality worship, a caring church, service to others, and faith maturity in peers. "If a congregation seeks to strengthen its impact on faith and loyalty," the study concluded, "involving members of all ages in quality Christian education is essential."[4]

MEANING THROUGH CHRISTIAN EDUCATION

We found that bonding churches have strong Christian education programs. Their members are more likely than members of high-loss churches to express satisfaction with church school classes for adults, with Bible study groups, and with church officer training. Chapter 9 will deal with programs for children and families. Here we look at programs for adults.

Trinity Church is located in a residential area of a stagnant city of fifty-five thousand on the eastern plains of middle America. In nine years it has grown from 750 to twelve hundred members because of its preaching and quality worship, its family-oriented programming, and its emphasis on Christian education. A strong adult education program covers a broad range of subjects that appeal to members with diverse backgrounds.

More than 250 members teach in one of the congregation's Christian education programs. A dynamic director of Christian education coordinates the educational offerings and develops lay leadership. Education for all ages is the order of the day on Sunday morning between two worship services. About two hundred adults participate regularly in courses requiring limited time commitments of from one to fourteen weeks.

On Wednesday evening about a hundred engage in serious Bible study requiring extended periods of commitment. This includes a Bethel Bible Series course, Kerygma Bible study, and an advanced Disciples course for potential Bible teachers.

On different weeknights small groups of up to fifteen people meet in members' homes. They use the Serendipity Bible study material and break into subgroups of about five people for discussion. These times of sharing build relationships, strengthen fellowship, and encourage members in their faith.

The pastor of Trinity Church estimates that about half their members are in one of their educational programs or small groups.

VARIED ADULT EDUCATION OPPORTUNITIES

Obviously there are many options for adult Christian education. Here we summarize a few that we found in bonding churches.

SHORT THEMATIC COURSES

These courses, which may last from one to twelve weeks, include such sub-jects as "Active Parenting," "Assertiveness," "Codependency: The Prodigal Child," "Seven Habits of Highly Effective People," "Christian Caregiving" (a sample lesson from the Stephen Ministry training course), "Know What You Believe," "The New Age and the Christian's Response," and "A Celebration of Christmas."

SHORT BIBLE COURSES BY BOOK OR BY THEME

THE BETHEL BIBLE SERIES is a two-year overview of the Bible designed to develop or refresh biblical literacy. It helps the Bible become "user friendly." Each lesson involves a one-hour lecture followed by discussion. It is usually offered on a weeknight in units of seven weeks. Persons can commit themselves for these limited periods, drop out, and return later for units they missed.

When Trinity Church started the Bethel series they prayed for twenty people, and forty-six showed up. They have used the Bethel series for several years. Now they have several hundred members who have completed the course and developed a love for the scriptures. The pastor says, "It ceases to be a program and becomes a way of life."

BIBLE DISCOVERY, like the Uniform Lesson material, covers all the Bible texts over a seven-year period, so it provides breadth and scope. It is a useful curriculum when a congregation wants to coordinate preaching and teaching because all age groups study the same biblical texts.

KERYGMA covers the major themes of the Old and New Testaments. It emphasizes discussion. People commit themselves to two hours of class and one-and-a-half hours of homework each week for thirty-three weeks a year.

SERENDIPITY is a program for small-group study that guides lay discussion leaders. It provides suggested approaches and extensive questions, printed opposite each page of the full Bible text. It combines learning and sharing of life experiences and perspectives.

DENOMINATIONAL CURRICULA help people understand the heritage and mission thrusts of their particular denomination. For Presbyterian and Reformed churches, there is *Bible Discovery,* mentioned above.

Some bonding churches have developed their own curriculum, using materials from various sources. Whatever the curriculum, we found that adult education must help members find meaning for living. Like preaching, it must relate biblical materials to the issues of life and death that members face. The *Effective Christian Education* study confirms this:

Effective content for both the adult and adolescent programs blends biblical knowledge and insight with significant engagement in the major life issues each age group faces. To a certain extent, these life issues have a value component in which one is called upon to make decisions. For adolescents, the issues include sexuality, chemical use, and friendship. For adults, they include global, political, and social issues, and issues related to cultural diversity.[5]

SMALL CHURCH ALTERNATIVES

Obviously, very small churches cannot simultaneously offer a broad range of educational options. However, through careful planning and the development of lay leadership, they can offer a varied program of short-term courses at different times throughout the year. And they also have the potential advantage of tailor-making programs to specific expressed concerns.

Beyond that they can join other nearby churches in joint education events. For the past twelve years the churches in one town have sponsored an annual school of theology. Imported leaders and local pastors lead three Monday-night workshops on some subject such as "Evangelism Within the Church" or "Alcoholism."

MEANING FOR MEN

The *Effective Christian Education* study tells us that men have a special need to develop both a strong vertical relationship with God and a strong horizontal relationship of service to others.

One pastor works at this through a focused ministry to men. Every Monday and Tuesday noon from September through May, "Sons of God" meet for lunch with the pastor. Monday is for men under forty years of age; Tuesday is for men over forty. The pastor gives a fifteen-minute devotion based on a biblical passage that throws light on a common concern of men. Being a father or an employer or working with a boss are examples. When a man joins the church, the pastor takes him to lunch one-on-one and gets him involved in one of the lunch groups.

Other congregations have men's breakfasts for Bible study, prayer groups, or other activities that aim to meet special needs of businessmen.

MEANING FOR WOMEN

Women's programs are noted for their capacity to educate and involve women in mission outreach. Bible study is an important part of most programs.

The annual retreat for the women of Trinity Church is a time of spiritual growth and inspiration. Planning begins a year in advance. The new planning group evaluates the past retreat and chooses a theme such as "Transforming Friendship" or "Spiritual Gifts." With the help of the director of Christian education, they select a study book on the theme. In preparation they themselves regularly study and pray together. At the retreat there are presentations, singing, times of fun, and quiet times. Each member of the planning committee leads a small group where women discuss the theme and share related life experiences.

MEANING THROUGH PRAYER AND RENEWAL PROGRAMS

Prayer chains, prayer groups, retreats, and renewal programs give meaning to many in bonding churches. Two examples show why.

Members of Suburban First Church remember the first of their annual spiritual renewal weekends. It was a time of deepened commitment for many. Presbytery staff members planned the program, which began on Saturday morning and closed Sunday afternoon. Some members arrived at the nearby synod camp on Friday evening. Others commuted. About a hundred people were divided into intergenerational *families* of from ten to twelve people each. Church members provided leadership for each family group as they engaged in Bible study, introspection, and consideration of the church's spiritual life. At times adults, young people, and children met in separate groups.

On Saturday night they had an old-fashioned revival meeting in a big tent with gospel hymns and the pastor preaching. Perhaps the high point of the weekend was the closing communion service on Sunday morning. They made an effort to get all members of the church to attend. Transportation was arranged to make that possible.

Some time before that, a couple had lost their eleven-year-old son, their only child, through tragic circumstances. "Why did a loving God allow this to happen?" they cried in anguish. Their church attendance lapsed. The pastor and a Stephen minister sought to help. The whole congregation got involved. Finally the couple adopted a daughter and brought her to the closing communion service for baptism. Before the baptism the father got up and said, "You know what we've been through. You've been through it with us. We still have questions, but we are coming here this morning to express our faith in spite of it all."

Members of Trinity Church look back four years to a four-day renewal program. It was a turning point in their congregational life. A visiting team led evening worship services on Thursday through Saturday and a closing service on Sunday. There were special breakfasts and two lunches, one for women and one for men. Members were assigned to small groups for study and sharing. "We received so much, we all wanted more," said one businessman. Out of those days of renewal grew a Bible study group of twenty-three men. They meet for breakfast each Saturday for study and sharing. Trinity's small-group ministry began then. When we visited, there were seven such groups meeting weekly either on Monday or Friday nights. A new group was about to start on Thursday nights.

CULTIVATE SMALL COMMUNITIES OF MEANING

To bond its members, a congregation must cultivate small caring communities where fellowship opens the door to pilgrimage in faith. Faith development takes place best within communities of trust. There people feel safe to talk openly about specific concerns in their lives. Together they learn how to relate their faith to those concerns. People need opportunities to question their faith. They grow through relationships where they dare to risk honest expression of doubts and fears. So a congregation must find ways to develop those small communities of trust throughout its life.

Lyle Schaller advocates quality small-group life as a key to assimilation.[6] Social scientists confirm this emphasis. They tell us that small groups give people opportunities to identify with other individuals and with a larger group. In small groups they can partially appropriate group values for themselves.

In *Congregations Alive* we described Pleasant Lake Church as a model of small-group ministry. At that time it had twenty-one hundred members with fifty koinonia groups of eight or more members each. These groups meet twice a month. They study the Bible or Christian literature and apply what they are studying to their own faith journeys. They pray together, share their concerns, experience caring love, and learn to care for others.[7]

In that congregation we discovered two keys to the success of the koinonia groups. First, the lay coordinators who lead the groups receive extensive training and use a syllabus. Second, the church requires all new members, regardless of their previous church experience, to participate for six weeks in an inquirer's group of up to fourteen members. These groups are very similar to koinonia groups but are geared to the spiritual needs of new members. This gives them a firsthand experience of Christian community.

Most new members have never used scripture themselves and do not know how to talk about their faith. Many have experienced the church as institution but not as Christian community. For many, this is the first time in their lives that they have discussed the relationship of their faith to their lives. About 80 percent of the inquirer's groups continue as koinonia groups.

Pleasant Lake Church is located in a suburban community with a high rate of turnover. Yet it emerged in our recent study as a church with one of the denomination's best records of membership retention. Ten years after our first study, it now has more than twenty-nine hundred members and at least sixty koinonia groups with a total of six hundred to seven hundred participants. In addition, there may be as many as thirty or forty groups that have arisen spontaneously.

The exciting development in this dynamic congregation is the way in which a small-group approach has now permeated all aspects of their program. "People are hungry and thirsty for Christian community," the pastor explains.

> We have much more diversity of life circumstances in our congregation now than we did ten years ago. So it is a big challenge to enable our members to find meaning and to grow in their faith. We find that small sharing groups are the key to such growth. They have helped the church to become a supporting family to those who need it so desperately.

In a variety of ways the church exposes members to brief, intimate, sharing experiences. They hope that busy people will discover how important it is to give koinonia groups priority in their crowded lives. For example, twice a year for three successive Saturdays about two hundred men meet for one-and-a-half hours. At each table eight or ten men are led into an experience of sharing their faith journeys with one another. They are then invited to continue as koinonia groups. Out of the last such event four koinonia groups with about twenty-four men decided to continue.

Adult education on Sunday morning is offered in modules of thirteen weeks. About three hundred men and women of all ages spend an hour together, again sitting around tables. First one of the pastors interprets some aspect of the Christian faith. Then a lay person tells how that aspect of faith is meaningful in his or her life. Then for thirty minutes people around each table talk over their faith journeys.

SMALL CHURCHES NEED SMALL GROUPS

Because small churches create natural friendships, some conventional wisdom implies they do not need any other small-group life. This is not true.

Most small churches already have subgroups that have formed naturally over the years. Women's circles, an adult Sunday school class, an adult fellowship group, or the choir—all can grow beyond relatively superficial friendliness to deeper mutual support in faith development. This can happen when someone gives them guidance, provides spiritual resources, and develops their skills.

Beyond that, however, we found small bonding churches that have developed successful koinonia-type groups. The sixty-six members of Hope Church suddenly found themselves in the midst of a development of ten thousand homes within commuting distance of a large city. In three years they have grown from a small country church to an actively caring community of 160 members. Their Sunday attendance is almost equal to their membership.

Most members do not have relatives in the area. So the intimate relationships they develop in the church help create a strong sense of family in the congregation. Faced with a high turn-over rate in the community, the church aims for the rapid incorporation of new members. They work hard to involve all members in small groups that enhance fellowship and support. As soon as possible they include them in the decision making of the church.

The congregation has capitalized on the potential friendship bonds of a small church. Members participate in two adult fellowship groups, one for those under forty and one for older folk. There is an adult church school class and a women's group. The choir has become a support group. Members have become involved in each other's lives.

A koinonia group of up to sixteen members meets weekly in one of the member's homes. After refreshments and a chance to "check in with one another," they study a book as stimulus for discussion and faith sharing.

A word of caution is appropriate at this point. A single focus on one's own spiritual growth and on the discovery of meaning for one's own satisfaction can be self-centered. Those who seek to save their lives lose them. Those that lose their lives for others find them. The discovery of meaning also demands an outward flow of energy to others. We examine this in our next chapter. Bonding churches serve others and shape society.

QUESTIONS FOR STUDY AND DISCUSSION

1. What is your best guess as to the proportion of your members who would say they find meaning for living in the activities of your congregation? In what activities do they discover that meaning? Where do you find meaning for living?

2. How strong is your adult Christian education program? What proportion of your adult members are involved in some form of study? How many are involved in Bible study? In what kinds of study? In Bethel Bible series? In Kerygma? In use of your denomination's curriculum materials? How effective do you feel these programs are in helping members find meaning for living?

3. In what ways does your preaching relate to your Christian education curriculum? If there are no discernable relationships, would there be an advantage in relating them? How might you do that in your congregation?

4. Do you believe that retreats or renewal programs are valuable ways to help members grow in their faith? Why or why not? Does your church have retreats for its total membership? How often? How effective do you judge them to be? Do groups within your church have retreats or renewal programs? What might you do to involve more members in such activities?

5. What kinds of small groups do you have in your congregation? Do they provide opportunities for members to build trust relationships? Are people able to share their doubts and their life concerns? Would a koinonia group be helpful to some members? How might you get it started?

RESOURCES

Benson, Peter L., and Carolyn H. Eklin. *Effective Christian Education: A National Study of Protestant Congregations—A Summary Report on Faith, Loyalty, and Congregational Life.* Minneapolis: Search Institute, 1990.

————. *Effective Christian Education Video Series.* Minneapolis: Search Institute, 1990. Search Institute, 22 West Franklin, Suite 525, Minneapolis, MN 55404-9835. (800) 888-7828.

The Bethel Series. P.O. Box 8398, Madison, WI 53708.

Bible Discovery. Presbyterian Publishing House, 100 Witherspoon Street, Louisville, KY 40202-1396. (800) 554-4694.

The Kerygma Program. 300 Mount Lebanon Boulevard, Suite 205, Pittsburgh, PA 15234. (412) 344-6062.

Serendipity. P.O. Box 1012, Littleton, CO 80160. (800) 525-9563.

Smith, Donald P. *Congregations Alive.* Philadelphia: Westminster Press, 1981.

5

SERVE OTHERS
AND SHAPE SOCIETY

The Spirit of the Lord . . . has anointed me
to bring good news to the poor. . . .
release to the captives
and recovery of sight to the blind,
to let the oppressed go free. . . .

LUKE 4:18

Service helps give meaning for living, deepens faith commitment, and encourages congregational loyalty. Members of bonding churches are more likely than members of high-loss churches to serve actively in the community, either through church-sponsored programs or through secular voluntary agencies. They are more likely to take the initiative in identifying needs and proposing ways to serve. Yet their community activities enhance their commitment to the church and do not interfere with church participation. This is equally true for small as for large churches.

The *Effective Christian Education* study makes a strong case for serving others and shaping society:

> The experience of serving others, through acts of mercy, compassion, or the promotion of social justice, is an important influence on the deepening of faith. The research evidence suggests that many youth and adults are uninvolved in such actions. Some of the best religious education occurs in these moments of giving, of connection, of bonding to others. Service needs to be a cornerstone of educational programming, partly because it is educationally-rich, and ultimately because, as people of faith, we are called to serve.[1]

A hundred-member church in the heart of a large Midwestern city has a blue-collar constituency. Its members discover meaning through their understanding of a call to ministry and their involvement in service. They are excited about their church. "It's a fun place to be," the pastor reports. "They want to be in mission."

It was not always so. When the pastor began his ministry there, discouragement hung heavily in the air. They asked, "How much time do we have left?" Repeatedly from the pulpit and in Bible study he teaches them, "As disciples, God calls you to ministry and mission. That means working for others."

In his preaching the pastor speaks to members' loneliness, anger, and hostility, and to other personal concerns. With his leadership, people discover how to live out their faith through service. In worship they celebrate their ministries. The pastor affirms from the pulpit specific ways members are serving others. "People need to hear what they are doing," he says.

Now, several years later, members have a new understanding of their identity as a congregation. "We are people in mission in a multiracial neighborhood," they say. The church is the center of their lives. There they are accepted, cared for, and given opportunities to use their energies in service to others.

Every third Sunday, members of the church serve in an ecumenical food pantry. A dinner for the neighborhood on the third Wednesday of every month draws as many as 150 people. Two men in their seventies do the cooking, and other members serve the food. A project that started as a fund-raiser has become an important community ministry. A pancake breakfast raises money for the community Little League. Members work in the neighborhood free health clinic. The pastor leads the way by serving on the board of the nonsectarian neighborhood house. On behalf of the church, he manages a "Needy Fund," which provides emergency relief. Thus the church helps a woman replace her broken windshield or provides bus transportation for the needy.

WAYS TO MEN'S HEARTS

Involving men in a service project can be one of the most effective ways to invite them into the life of the church. An active member of Broadview Church told of his pilgrimage away from the church and back again:

> Years ago I left another church because I saw members say one thing and do another. They would solicit a temperance pledge on Sunday and get drunk on Monday. I returned to *this* church through the back door. Someone in the men's brotherhood asked me to do some repair jobs. Then, when the men got together each month and cooked their own

supper, I joined them. Now I meet with some of those men in the prayer breakfast group. It means a lot to me to serve by teaching a Bible class. Nobody could run me off now. My commitment is to Christ and to the church.

Retired men in a Thursday noon Bible class at Trinity Church bring their lunch and study for half an hour. Many of them come early or stay after lunch to cut the grass and help the custodian with repairs. They move tables and chairs and do other inside jobs.

WHAT ENCOURAGES INVOLVEMENT IN SERVICE

The extent of members' participation in service depends on several factors:

An understanding of ministry as being the work of all the people and a commitment to working out its implications.

Biblical and theological convictions that emphasize personal faith journeys, compassion, social justice, and social action.

A firm conviction that all members have gifts, coupled with a commitment to identify, develop, and use those gifts in significant service.

A caring pastor who convincingly calls members to ministry and captures their imagination with specific ways to serve.

Recognition of specific needs by caring individuals or groups.

Leadership that responds to needs as they arise and expects members to participate in service to others.

A climate of freedom that allows individuals or groups to use their creativity in meeting needs.

Organization of volunteer resources to identify members' interests, abilities, and gifts, and to channel them into service.

Public recognition by the congregation of those who involve themselves in volunteer services.

Willingness of leadership to work with other churches and community organizations to meet community needs.

USING THE GIFTS GOD HAS GIVEN

The secret to involving members in significant service to others is to focus on gifts. God gives the church the gifts it needs to fulfill its mission in the world. Those gifts are not given to only a few persons. They are present in an amazing variety in all members of a congregation. If every member of the body is gifted, then every member has the capacity to carry out some helpful ministry.

Members want to serve and to make use of their gifts. All they need is a good opportunity to do so. Recruiting fails when the church asks them to do jobs that do not match their interests, skills, or experience. The ardor of activists cools when we expect them to sit in committee meetings rather than to accomplish a task that uses their gifts. Give them jobs to do. On the other hand, some members are gifted in planning, organizing, and delegating tasks to others. Let those members chair committees and serve on them.

Our calling as church leaders is to

identify members' gifts,

help people recognize their giftedness,

convince members of their importance to the work of the kingdom,

cultivate members' gifts,

match them to opportunities for ministry,

support them with training and needed resources, and

celebrate ways in which members are using their gifts.

This means that people are more important than programs. The focus is on the gifts they bring rather than on finding staff for existing activities. Wherever possible, program responds to gifts that God gives. Mission groups grow out of concerns and visions that individuals bring to the church. Committees and task forces arise out of the life of the congregation.

Leaders listen and respond. They suggest opportunities for service and watch for ways to channel interest into active ministry. This calls for a delicate orchestration of the needs of the community, a vision of mission, the gifts of individuals, and responsiveness to their initiatives. Such responsiveness allows the Spirit of God to move with initiatives from the most unlikely sources.

CHANNELING GIFTS TO OPPORTUNITIES FOR SERVICE

One congregation with a membership of about 325 members has an average Sunday worship attendance equal to about half its members. It makes a concerted effort to involve them in service activities. Once a year the commitment committee of session asks all members to fill out a time and talent survey. They then update the church's computer and pass information on to session committees. The volunteer coordinator of their "Connecting Links" program has an exceptional gift for organization. She uses the survey to set up service subgroups. These respond to members' needs for transportation, home repair, or help with taxes and business concerns.

Other churches use a pattern derived from Marlene Wilson's helpful book, *How to Mobilize Church Volunteers*. A part-time paid volunteer coordinates the program. Organizations carefully define jobs that need to be done. All groups prepare a mission statement. Trained volunteers interview members of the congregation to identify their gifts. What are they doing now? What would they like to do? What do they *not* want to do? What are they trained to do? The coordinator makes certain that someone follows up to recruit members for appropriate jobs and to give them the training, resources, and support they need. Such follow-up is essential.

"Time and talent sheets have helped officially reject people's gifts every year," Marlene Wilson states. A church should never collect them unless it uses them. When we do not call on people, it tells them that their gifts are not valuable or that we do not need them. "Many pew-sitters have received that message very clearly."[2]

Effective programs update the roster of members' interests and gifts at least every year. Then follow up. One congregation puts a full page of service opportunities in each Sunday's bulletin. They estimate that 80 percent of their members take part in the ministries of the church.

RECOGNIZE THOSE WHO SERVE

People appreciate appreciation. A congregation of about one hundred has an average fall worship attendance of ninety. It emphasizes services of recognition. At Christmas, Easter, and Thanksgiving services they recognize by name individuals in the congregation who serve the church or the community. Each year they commission their Sunday school workers.

Broadview Church has a special recognition luncheon for volunteers and has a bulletin board on which it posts pictures of volunteers at work.

HOW CONGREGATIONS SERVE OTHERS

Ways in which bonding churches involve their members in service seem almost endless. They create programs of their own and work in joint projects with other churches. They give to and participate in community organizations, and they make their facilities available to groups that meet community needs. We offer the following descriptions as stimuli to churches that want to increase their members' involvement in service.

CONGREGATIONAL SERVICE PROGRAMS

THE ANNUAL CHRISTMAS FAMILIES PROGRAM seeks to bring holiday joy to several low-income families. Nearby schools identify some families in the free-lunch program. Each year the church selects a different set of families. Deacons visit the families in advance of Christmas to learn about them and their situation. They find out about children who are not of school age. A letter in English and in Spanish explains why the church members want to share their Christmas joy with each family. A few days before Christmas the deacons bring boxes of food and a twenty-dollar gift certificate for a clothing store. There are toys for the children and a Spanish or English Bible.

A MISSION FAIR one Sunday after church provides booths for community service organizations. They interpret their work and recruit volunteers. Included are a center for transients and the homeless, a home for unwed mothers, a prison mission, a resettlement organization, alternative Christmas giving, and a marriage encounter program. Extensive advertising draws people from the whole community. Hot dogs, chili, and craft displays add to the attraction.

EMERGENCY RELIEF. People in one community lost everything in a big flood. Members of a nearby church gave household goods to members of a church in the flooded area. Later the two congregations got together for a big barbecue to celebrate their closer relationship.

A MINISTRY FOR THE HOMELESS helps feed those who are not eligible for help from other organizations. For example, the rescue mission will not help those who are drunk. Each Sunday after church a core of about twenty volunteers gathers in the church kitchen. They prepare 250 bag lunches. Volunteers then distribute them to the shanties where the homeless live. Sometimes they also bring clothes or blankets. Some of the homeless attend church and stay after the service to help make the sandwiches.

Cooperative Ecumenical Projects

Reach out is a joint endeavor of many churches. It serves the needs of low-income, elderly, and disabled persons. The coordinated skills of four hundred volunteers give services that other agencies do not provide. They do grocery shopping for a blind lady twice a month, provide transportation twice a week for a woman who needs kidney dialysis treatments, or do laundry for a woman who is recovering from an operation. A handyman repairs the front steps of an elderly woman's home and cleans her gutters. Volunteers make meals, clean houses, tutor, and visit in nursing homes and prisons. As needed, they make referrals to agencies.

Loaves and fishes provides nourishing meals each noon to senior citizens. Volunteers serve meals in the basement fellowship hall of Covenant Church. The church, along with other neighboring churches, subsidizes food costs.

Love church services network uses volunteers to screen those who need social services. Under supervision of a paid director, they do intake interviews and weed out those who are abusing the system. They encourage congregations to tithe their talents as well as their money. Each church keeps a talent survey, which the network can draw on.

Project home again helps homeless families rent their own homes. Each church sponsors one or two families and negotiates the details of their mutual relationship. It provides their first three months' rent and a damage deposit and helps them get settled. One church found housing for a single mother with four young children. Later, she enrolled in one of its new member classes.

A *battered-family shelter* began as a project of one church with the cooperation of several others. When a broad base of support developed, they spun it off as a community responsibility. The original church continues as one of the participating groups. One of the church's members is the director.

Other interfaith programs might include

    providing meals and temporary shelter for the homeless in different churches for two weeks at a time;

    a bargain clothing center that sells donated clothes for a few cents apiece;

a food pantry, or

providing volunteers and funds for Habitat for Humanity.

SERVICE THROUGH COMMUNITY ORGANIZATIONS

FISH is an ecumenical lay volunteer service movement widespread in communities across the country. It generally seeks to serve particular needs of the community not being served by other agencies. This varies from one locale to another. In the area served by Covenant Church, *FISH Emergency Service, Inc.,* provides food, clothing, and referral assistance to persons who cannot get basic necessities because of ill health, loss of a job, or other problems. Many clients are single parents with young children. Covenant Church has a Fish Sunday when members contribute needed goods.

A HOME FOR WOMEN with chemical or drug dependencies and their children receives support from groups in Covenant Church.

USE OF FACILITIES BY OUTSIDE GROUPS

Some churches pride themselves on the use of their facilities by other service groups. Broadview Church identified sixty or seventy groups and boasts that they have become a kind of community center. People know them as the church that cares about the community.

In bonding churches we found such groups as Alcoholics Anonymous, Al-Anon, Parents Anonymous, and recovery groups for patients discharged from mental hospitals. They house senior citizens programs, Meals on Wheels, Parents' Day Out, Parents Without Partners, Boy Scouts, Girl Scouts, or Campfire Girls. One church has an after-school-care program for elementary school children through the sixth grade sponsored by the town's board of education.

CHURCHES HELP TO SHAPE THEIR COMMUNITY

Members of bonding churches are often influential in shaping their communities. They serve on boards of community agencies, are members of school boards, serve on town councils, or carry significant responsibilities as executives of such bodies.

Broadview Church has a comprehensive program of service to its community. Members serve in community organizations. A part-time staff member coordinates volunteer activities. Their extensive adult Christian education program has a strong emphasis on Bible study. Members of their evangelism committee knock on doors in the community. However, it was their emphasis on social action that attracted the woman who directs their children's choirs:

> I am here because I wanted a quality Christian education program and good youth groups for our children. I also was seeking a church and society committee that was dealing with critical social issues. I am deeply concerned with the improvement of public education, with the environment, and with women's issues.
>
> Our congregation has been able to deal with such explosive matters as reproductive freedom for women. This is because we work hard to respect each other and our differing points of view. We try to persuade one another and really to be open to dialogue. You know where people stand on the issues, but that doesn't become a barrier to our relationships.
>
> I attribute this to the ministerial leadership we have had over the years. They have a clear sense of commitment to Christ and to the congregation. They exude a genuine regard for people. They encourage different approaches. Though you may not agree with them, or with each other, they accept you. They spend one-on-one time with people and have the flexibility to share leadership with others.
>
> After all, if we can't deal with explosive issues as Christians, how can we expect others to deal with them?

In line with its broad approach, this church includes in its budget both Planned Parenthood and Emergency Infancy Services. It spent considerable time and effort to study and promote a major educational reform bill that was pending in the state legislature. The law resulted in reducing class sizes in the schools and increasing teachers' salaries.

ADVOCACY OF SOCIAL ISSUES

Advocacy for social issues can either be divisive or stimulating of vitality depending on how churches handle it. The literature suggests that social action relates positively to a church's growth if it does not generate conflict and disunity, and if it relates to ultimate meanings as understood and accepted by its members. Experience tells me that pastoral care of the flock helps people listen patiently to their pastor whether or not they agree with him or her.

Joe Brown is pastor of a hundred-member congregation in a conservative farm community in the north central United States. He takes strong stands on social issues that often lead to sharp disagreement with some members. Yet their fall worship attendance averages ninety members. There are twelve senior high and seven junior high young people in the youth groups. The church has three choirs. During his seven-year ministry, the congregation has built a Sunday school addition and has moved from dependence on mission aid to self-support. Their mission giving has gone up from 1 percent of their local budget to 10 percent. Session members tell us that most members find deep meaning for daily living in their congregational experience. They say the pastor clearly articulates that meaning.

Two things have made all this possible. First is the authenticity of Joe Brown's own struggle to be faithful as he faces the issues he advocates. Second is the compassionate, caring ministry he exercises in the lives of people in his parish. The pastor explains, "They see me as a challenger. I live deeply what I believe, and people recognize that. I preach from the lectionary and give personal examples out of my own faith journey. I struggle too—with many of the same things they struggle with."

When the congregation called Pastor Brown, they made it clear that they expected him to involve himself actively in the community. When he is not ministering to his other yoked congregation, he has almost constant contact with his people. Living in a small community with a small congregation has its advantages.

Almost every day Pastor Brown eats lunch in the upper elementary school with church members who are on its staff. He coaches the high school girls' track team, the debate team, and the quiz bowl team. He has been instrumental in organizing a scholastic achievement council, which gives awards for academic achievement and citizenship. He goes to the high school basketball games, joins senior citizens in their luncheons, and accompanies church young people on their outings.

Early in his ministry, a small Bible study group of parents and children was studying peacemaking. They identified a community problem concerning school property taxes. This sparked the first of several open forums on volatile issues sponsored by the church.

After a visit to Nicaragua, Joe Brown arranged for another open forum. This time it was on Nicaragua. In a Sunday sermon he gave his reasons for objecting to our national policy there. Immediately after the sermon, which comes near the middle of their service, a leading elder of the congregation rose abruptly and left the sanctuary. "At the potluck lunch that followed," the pastor says, "he confronted me publicly. He let me have it!"

Soon after that, the elder's son was home on a visit. At 2 A.M. Pastor Brown's phone rang. The elder's son had just received word that his wife had been killed in an accident. Immediately the pastor and his wife went to the elder's home. They spent much of the rest of the night with the family, comforting, reading scripture, and praying. They helped arrange air transportation for the family. Next morning Joe Brown called a pastor in the city where the tragedy had occurred, asking him to minister to the family in their loss. Meanwhile he and his wife took care of the elder's home during his absence.

Two weeks later the elder and his wife returned. During the announcement period on Sunday morning, Pastor Brown welcomed them back. The elder rose and spoke to the whole congregation. "I am sure that none of you are aware of what Joe Brown has done for me and my family. As you all know, we disagree with each other on policy issues. But we do not disagree on our faith. And he is my pastor."

The Positive Power of Social Action

Social action can draw members into deeper involvement. An African American congregation with well over two hundred members is located in an inner city neighborhood of the South. The congregation tried to get a young adult group going but failed. They talked of various recreational possibilities such as tennis or bowling. No interest! Their most successful attempt to involve young adults resulted from a new effort to be of service to the community. They plan to adopt a street in the neighborhood. They hope to help people care for their apartments and clean up their yards. The first step in the program involved about fifteen members, mostly young married couples. They volunteered to visit in the neighborhood as the first step in this community development effort. Community service proved to be the key that unlocked deeper member involvement.

To the Ends of the Earth

Congregations that seek to involve their members in a full-orbed approach to service reach out to the whole world of need. Some do this by participating in such well-known international service programs as the Heifer Project, CARE, CROP Walk, UNICEF, and the One Great Hour of Sharing and Witness Offering.

Covenant Church installed an elevator to make its buildings accessible to the disabled. In its fund-raising campaign it included the feeding of destitute families in its neighborhood, a national missions building project in Alaska, and a medical van to serve twenty-seven rural communities in India.

The pastor of a small congregation whose elderly members actively care for one another encourages international outreach through giving to mission programs. One year they hung a paper chain around the sanctuary. They called it a "Chain of Love." Each link represented a dollar given by some member of the church to a school, hospital, or other project in some other part of the world. "This chain is God's love surrounding us," the pastor reminded his people each week as he described for them the mission of the month to which they were giving.

SUMMARY

What does it take to draw tightly the bonds of commitment to Christ and the church? We have seen that members are drawn into the church when

responsive churches open themselves to the winds of the Spirit,

compassionate communities meet diverse needs and care for one another in all life's circumstances,

small groups study, pray, and grow together, as they discover meaning on life's pilgrimage, and

people of God reach out to a world of need.

More is also required. New members must move quickly from the fringes of congregational life toward its center. They need to feel that they really belong. Bonding churches incorporate members diligently.

QUESTIONS FOR STUDY AND DISCUSSION

1. Do you agree that involvement in service to others is important for faith development? If not, why not? If so, what proportion of your members do you estimate are actively involved in serving others?

2. In what ways is your congregation involved in service to one another? What programs or organizations of the church involve members in serving the community? In what ways do members as individuals engage in community service?

3. In what ways is your church involved in studying the social issues of your community or city? Of the nation? Of the world? In what ways are you involved in social action to shape society? Why or why not?

4. What might your congregation do to increase its involvement in social service or social action?

RESOURCES

Smith, Donald P. *Congregations Alive.* Philadelphia: Westminster Press, 1981.

Wilson, Marlene. *How To Mobilize Church Volunteers.* Minneapolis: Augsburg Publishing House, 1983.

6

INCORPORATE MEMBERS DILIGENTLY

On vacation our family worshiped in a little country church in a new suburb. Two small boys greeted us in the parking lot. "You don't belong here," they said defiantly.

I tried to explain. "We thought we'd like to visit you," I said.

"We haven't seen you before!" they insisted. This was *their* church, and strangers were not welcome.

Adult church members would never think of giving a visitor such a greeting. But many a visitor in many a church has felt the way those little boys tried to make us feel. We did not belong. But belonging is an essential ingredient in the retention of church members. And the incorporation of visitors and new members into congregational life is critically important to their bonding. Churches can incorporate new members effectively by

caring about them as visitors,

carefully preparing them for membership,

clearly articulating high expectations for them,

clarifying their expectations of the church, its ministers, and its staff,

enlisting their participation in activities beyond the Sunday worship services,

identifying, developing, and using their gifts in significant service,

giving them opportunities to shape the program of the congregation,

providing diligent pastoral care early in their membership.

THE COURTSHIP OF VISITORS

The initial impulse toward belonging can come with the first contacts a visitor has with the church. First impressions draw them closer to the congregation or make them feel more distant.

At Westminster Church one volunteer has a passion for recruiting and training ushers and greeters. He likes to say, "Every person in the world, every day, wears a sign that says *I need to feel important!* Greeters and ushers can help visitors feel that way. Call people by name if you know it. With visitors, give your name and say, 'I don't believe we've met.' Ushers need to take charge. Without a word, people are saying, 'Take care of me. Make me feel comfortable, and seat me where I want to sit.'"

Some churches recruit new members as greeters. This way they can ask for people's names without embarrassment. Meanwhile they will be getting acquainted. Name tags are helpful if you can get members to wear them. Some congregations that do not regularly use name tags have a "Name Tag Day." Everyone, including old members, wears a tag.

In Covenant Church at the close of the service several greeters stand by the minister at the door. When visitors introduce themselves, a greeter offers to take them to the coffee hour. If they accept the invitation, the greeter introduces them to members with whom they may have something in common. This helps them feel comfortable.

A congregation is fortunate if it has someone who naturally spots strangers and welcomes them. Churches may wish to sensitize members to the importance of doing this. People in the helping professions or in sales work usually find it easy to get acquainted with strangers. Each month ask two or three of them to shepherd visitors during the coffee hour, helping them feel at home.

Such hosts should remember that people differ in their readiness for intimacy. Some make friends quickly. They welcome a warm and friendly greeting. Others prefer anonymity, especially in their first visit to a church. They may respond negatively to high pressure friendliness. They hesitate to be involved too quickly. This requires friendliness without smothering. It takes considerable skill and sensitivity to respond to each visitor with just the right mix of friendliness and space.

Visitors to Small Churches

In small churches like the hundred-member Plainfield Church several key people can make a big difference. With the pastor's encouragement, two members have taken the initiative to record attendance and get people involved in the church. The dynamic Bible teacher in that congregation had felt out of place in her previous church. Her commitment here is obvious:

> At last I felt at home spiritually. After a couple of visits, members called on the phone. I got three or four notes welcoming me. "We were glad to see you," they would say. There was no heavy recruitment. I felt welcomed out of an interest and concern for me and not because they needed another member. Young and old made me and my children feel at home.

ORGANIZING TO INCORPORATE VISITORS

Larger churches will need a more organized approach than that. Trinity Church, with nearly twelve hundred members, has been receiving between seventy-five and a hundred new members each year. It has been growing in spite of its location in a stable community. The church has carefully orchestrated a plan for incorporating visitors into the fellowship. They track attendance by passing friendship pads during the service and keep records on each new and regular visitor.

On a visitor's first Sunday, a couple from the congregation makes a friendly call. They stay no longer than five minutes and do not go into the house. Sunday is family time. They take a loaf of home-baked bread and a brochure, express a welcome, invite them back, and answer their questions. These outreach callers volunteer to visit on the same Sunday every month for a year. After church they gather the pads and identify first-time visitors. After their visit, they send a postcard.

Early in the first week the pastor sends a welcoming letter and an associate makes another brief call. He or she enters notes on the visitor's card or in a computer.

Volunteer "harvesters" receive training in two two-hour sessions. On the third Monday evening of the month they meet, get their assignments, and call on visitors. Their purpose is "to share the love of Jesus" and to listen for any special needs or concerns. Appropriate follow-up continues until the visitor joins the church or decides to affiliate with some other congregation.

PREPARING PROSPECTS FOR MEMBERSHIP

Most congregations prepare prospects for membership in some way. Classes vary in method and in length. Our study found that bonding churches are more likely to have classes that total from four to seven hours. High-loss churches are more likely to have classes that total from one to three hours.

Establishing a deep and lasting commitment to Christ and the church requires more than a conversation with the pastor or a brief meeting with the governing board. This calls for more than one short session.

Many churches structure new-member preparation as an inquirer's class. The pastor of a 270-member congregation with an average attendance of two hundred explains that they require the class. "People know they may come to learn about who we are and what we believe. They need not feel like they must make a premature decision to join."

Helpful content often includes:

A time of getting acquainted.

Exploring where potential members are in their faith pilgrimage and helping them grow in their commitment to Jesus Christ. Pastors begin by sharing their own faith journey and ask others to tell of theirs.

Orienting inquirers to the particular congregation, its program, form of government, and denominational heritage. Committee chairpersons may describe program opportunities. An interest inventory is often collected.

Communicating a summary of basic Christian doctrine and church history.

Giving an overview of community, world, and ecumenical mission.

Introducing inquirers to a small-group experience, which will lead to continued involvement in at least one small group.

Clarifying expectations that new members have of the church and its minister(s).

Communicating expectations that the congregation has of its members.

Giving inquirers an opportunity to decide whether this congregation will meet their needs and whether they want to make the commitments the church expects of them.

Classes may involve a presentation by the pastor and one or more lay leaders, followed by small-group interaction. We have mentioned that Pleasant Lake Church deliberately structures small inquirer's classes as an introduction to their extensive koinonia group ministry. Small classes allow for building relationships among inquirers and class leaders.

Depending on community patterns of life, an inquirer's class might take place on a Saturday or a Sunday afternoon and evening. It might be a series of classes on Sunday mornings or on some weeknight.

CLARIFYING EXPECTATIONS THAT MEMBERS BRING

All new members have expectations of the church, whether or not they are conscious of them. If the church is to meet their needs and win their loyalty, members need an opportunity to express those expectations.

During his inquirer's class, one pastor asks each new member their level of commitment to the church. Do they plan to attend worship every Sunday or less often? Are there circumstances that make regular attendance impossible? In what organizations or activities are they planning to participate? Are they willing to serve on a committee? He then seeks to put every willing member on a committee within six months of their joining the church. He maintains that this personal approach is much more effective than asking members to fill out an interest form and following up later.

This approach gets new-member expectations out into the open. It clarifies them as points of reference in pastoral care. Thus, when a member with an "every Sunday" commitment is absent for several Sundays, the pastor makes a phone call. He tells them he misses them and finds out how they are doing. About 25 percent of the time he finds problem situations that lead to a visit. If after the phone call a member does not appear at worship for two weeks, the pastor visits them. "If members are to stay involved," he asserts, "the minister must stay on top of it."

PREDICTING THE PINCHES

The inquirer's class provides an ideal time to develop patterns of communication that can lessen later unhealthy conflicts and loss of members. New members need to realize that some of their expectations of the church or its minister will not be met. John Savage calls those disappointments *pinches* and advocates urging new members to bring their pinches to the pastor or to a trained pinch hearer. Chapter 8 will describe this more fully.

THE VALUE OF HIGH EXPECTATIONS

There is an important advantage in requiring participation in an inquirer's class. It helps establish high expectations for membership. These can lead to strong commitment and bonding. Jesus had high expectations of his disciples. Why do we expect less? The temptation for most mainline churches is to make it too easy to join the church.

Market research has discovered that a product's sale price must relate to the buyer's perception of its value. It does not matter what it costs the seller. If people feel the price is too high, they will not buy because they believe the product is not worth the cost. If it is too low, people will not buy because they devalue the product. Could it be that one reason members drop out is that the church has never asked them to pay a high enough price?

Conservative denominations that are growing have stringent membership requirements and make heavy demands on their members. They are strict about faith formulas, about giving to the church, and about life-styles. They are even intolerant of others who differ from them. However, studies have shown that strictness does not characterize growing congregations in mainline denominations.

Rather than strictness, our studies suggest that high expectations do promote congregational vitality. Like the ministering churches in *Congregations Alive,* bonding churches clearly articulate their faith. They expect their members to take seriously the Christian faith and life that church membership implies. Members of bonding churches are more likely than members of high-loss churches to feel that the church has high expectations for their understanding of and commitment to the Christian faith. Pastors of bonding churches are more likely than pastors of high-loss churches to say that members of their churches have a clear sense of the congregation's purpose.

High expectations relate positively to worship attendance. We found that high-attendance churches are more likely than low-attendance churches to communicate to their new members the expectation that they witness to Christ through daily living. They expect members to participate in social service and to attend worship services.

One congregation tells its members that if they do not get involved in at least two activities other than the worship service, they will not grow in their church relationship.

HIGH EXPECTATIONS IN A SMALL CHURCH

We found that the larger the church, the more likely it will communicate its expectations that members support it with their time and talents. Yet, small bonding churches are more likely than small high-loss churches to communicate that expectation to their members. This suggests that small churches can magnify members' loyalty by expecting them to give their time to the church. Two pastors of small churches tell their stories:

> We are a small church. Everybody knows there are jobs for everyone. And everyone expects you to pull your load. Yes, that is part of being in a small town or even in a small congregation. But high expectations are especially true of this congregation. We have talented members. They have attained a high educational level. Most of them are elders or deacons because we have taken rotation of session membership seriously. One of our themes is *To whom much is given, much is expected.*

> I keep telling our members that the Christian life is a joyous life. However, it is also a life of obligation. When we receive new members, we expect them to involve themselves in one of the ministry groups through which the congregation carries on its work.

BREACHING THE BARRIERS TO INCLUSIVENESS

Lyle Schaller estimates that from one-third to one-half of all Protestant church members do not feel that they really belong to their congregations. They have never been accepted into the inner "fellowship circle." He says, "Frequently it is easier to become a member of a Protestant congregation than it is to be accepted into the fellowship of that community of believers."[1]

Schaller has identified an important dilemma for congregations that are trying to incorporate new members. The very qualities that bind a congregation together may keep new members out of the inner fellowship circle and lead to their dropping out. Congregational cohesiveness comes from some organizing principle. Schaller gives us a long list: ethnic language, denominational identity, the personality and magnetism of the minister, congregational life-style, meeting place, program, a unifying task, kinfolk ties, heritage, nostalgia, etc.[2] The more powerful the cohesive force, the more likely it will exclude newcomers.

Because many congregations may be completely unaware of these exclusionary forces, they need to identify what glues them together. They must discover ways they discourage others from becoming members or from becoming part of the inner fellowship circle.

Contrary to our expectations, we found that small high-loss churches are more likely than small bonding churches to feel that their congregation is like a warm, caring family. Congruent with Schaller's theory, we suspect that in those high-loss churches, veteran members so highly prize their strong sense of family that new members never really feel accepted. This leads to a high dropout rate.

NEW MEMBER SPONSORS

To help an inquirer's transition to full participation, some congregations link each of them to a sponsor with similar interests. Families sponsor families. Singles sponsor singles. A sponsor-inquirer pair attend the first two inquirer's classes together. Between the two classes the sponsor calls to see if the inquirer has any questions. A dinner together may help them get better acquainted. Older members are mentors for young people in the confirmation class.

After a member joins, the sponsor uses the Sunday coffee hour and other church functions as opportunities to introduce the new member to as many people as possible. Sponsors encourage new members to participate in a small group, a class, or an education event, and invite them to the next appropriate fellowship group or churchwide activity.

Three or four weeks after new members join the church, sponsors telephone or visit them to find out how things are going. They encourage involvement in activities, answer questions, and offer any other needed help.

When six months have elapsed, an ideal task for one of the new members is to serve as a sponsor for some other new member.

PLANNING FOR INCLUSION

One important antidote to member dropout is to plan carefully for the incorporation of new members. A United Presbyterian study of church membership growth found that growing congregations are more likely to have procedures for incorporating new members into the life of the congregation. These programs include more intensive training for membership and more use of new members in church life.

In contrast with this are the Alban Institute's conclusions from a study in sixteen congregations of different denominations. Those churches "had almost no formal assimilation systems whatsoever! For the most part what happened to help people become members was informal, unplanned, unsupervised, and unintentional."[3]

Our present study of six hundred Presbyterian congregations produced mixed results. Bonding and high-loss churches are equally likely to have planned procedures to incorporate new members into congregational life. About two-thirds of both groups have such procedures. Most of the churches use three methods:

1. Encouraging new members to join one of their small groups.

2. Inviting new members to accept some particular task.

3. Inviting new members to accept a committee assignment or an office in the congregation.

These are the three key elements that Lyle Schaller believes are essential to membership retention. If one or another of these does not happen within the first year, he says, members are likely to become inactive.[4]

Bonding and high-loss churches differ in the relative importance they give to the first of these methods. Bonding churches of all sizes are more likely than high-loss churches to encourage members to join one of their small groups.

Encouraging New Members to Join a Small Group

Our study confirms that small groups play a crucial role in membership bonding. We asked pastors to name three or four approaches to membership retention that have been especially helpful in their churches. Their most frequent response was small-group involvement. Members of bonding churches are more likely than members of high-loss churches to belong to three or more organizations, committees, or groups within their churches.

The pastor of a five-hundred-member congregation insists that incorporation takes place only through participation in some form of church school class or other small group experience. He feels so strongly about this that he is seriously weighing whether they should make such participation a requirement for church membership.

Ocean View Church encourages all new members to participate in some adult education class or group activity. Each Sunday when they receive new members, they have a mission fair in their courtyard or fellowship hall. They invite old members to attend. Each church group has a booth with brochures describing their activities. Interpreters at each booth answer questions and encourage people to sign up. This large and growing church has found this to be an excellent way to inform and enlist both new members and old.

Inviting New Members to Accept a Task

Session committees told us the most frequent approach they use to minimize dropouts is to give a job to everyone. This can be a task within the life of the congregation itself or involvement in some outreach ministry of the church.

Bonding churches are more likely than high-loss churches to have a laity Sunday. They are more likely to have special Sundays when women are responsible for the entire worship service. Many regularly involve laity as liturgists in worship services.

Inviting New Members to Accept an Office

Small bonding churches are more likely than small high-loss churches to invite new members to accept a committee assignment or an office in the congregation. In three years Hope Church has grown from sixty-six to 160 members. They have a weekly attendance close to 100 percent of the membership level. About 60 percent of its members belong to ministry groups that focus on different aspects of the congregation's life. They generate program ideas and carry them out after session approval. Each group consists of two elders and ten members from the congregation at large.

A congregation of two hundred members located in a relatively stable community in the eastern United States has been growing in membership. The pastor feels that one of the important ingredients in its retention of members is its policy to move new members into leadership positions as rapidly as possible. Their goal is to have two new teachers in the church school every year. They aim for a turnover in job positions (teachers, superintendent, women's circle officers, and committee chairs) every two or three years. The nominating committee now takes care to put new people into leadership positions. This gets them involved quickly in the life of the church, broadens the base of participation and gives long-standing members the opportunity to serve in new capacities or to take much-needed sabbaticals.

Involve Members in Decision Making

Involvement of members in decision making generates more satisfaction than participation alone. In voluntary associations, the amount of control that members exercise generally affects the level of their commitment. In America the church is a voluntary association among countless voluntary organizations from which a person may choose. Members must feel that they have some influence over those parts of church life that concern them. Otherwise they may become apathetic and leave for some other organization that includes them actively in its inner circle.

Congregations attract and keep members by involving them in shaping policies and programs in a manner appropriate to the polity of their denomination. Members will accept any necessary limitations if the congregation meets their expectations and is operating smoothly. If it does not, they will react negatively.

Growing congregations in a United Presbyterian study had a more inclusive and sensitive style of decision making than did declining congregations. They were more open to new ideas and approaches. Members affirmed that their sessions were more sensitive to the feelings of different parts of the congregation. Members mutually encouraged one another, offered each other new ideas for solving problems, and kept each other informed about important events and situations.

We found that bonding churches are more likely than high-loss churches to involve their members in decision making by representing different ages, interests, perspectives, and organizations on task forces and committees. The larger the church the more likely it is to use this method of involvement.

A downtown church with more than eight hundred members retains its members, among other reasons, because it involves them actively in the governance of the church. Since its formation by the merger of three congregations, it has affirmed and carried out a "co-ministry" style of leadership. The congregation rejected a hierarchical style and has called all four of its ordained ministers as co-pastors. There is a strong emphasis on lay ministry. Members make decisions by participating in twenty-one committees that guide and carry out the church's program.

Small churches involve members in decisions by asking for their opinions on various aspects of program and activities and by bringing new program or activity possibilities to congregational meetings for input or decision.

The session of one church described in *Congregations Alive*[5] gives a charter to each of its committees. The session approves budgets and sets policies. It then authorizes committees to plan and carry out programs without further action by the session. To maintain close liaison and insure coordination, a member of session sits with each committee. The pastor also meets with most major committees and works closely with their chairpersons.

A pastor in our present study says to his committees, "Don't come asking for permission. Just do it!

"Any group," he explains, "is going to be more creative than I am. I just need to get out of the way and steer them to the information they need."

The advantage of such a model is that it provides many opportunities for members to achieve psychological success. As defined by Kurt Lewin, people will feel successful when they choose their own goals, when they feel their goals are challenging and meaningfully related both to their self-concept and to the goals of the organization, when the means of reaching them have been self-determined, and when they achieve the goals.[6]

SABBATICALS SAVE VALUABLE LEADERS

We have said that the more actively members participate in the work of a congregation the more likely will be their congregational loyalty. There is one important exception. Devoted members may burn themselves out. They may be too active in leadership or service activities over long periods.

"Last year I was at overload," one active woman told us. "I dropped out of church. You can't be a nurturer unless you nurture yourself." "Sometimes I need to be needed as a leader," another told us. "But sometimes I need to rest and be restored." Congregations should legitimize sabbaticals for active members. This can avoid burnout and make it unnecessary for leaders to escape to anonymity in some other congregation.

A TIME FOR INTENSIVE PASTORAL CARE

A church of six hundred members in the Southeast has an average fall attendance equal to almost 60 percent of its members. It has a very active and well-integrated program to incorporate new members into its fellowship. Its principal focus is on pastoral care. The pastor's philosophy is clear:

> New members have the most instability in their lives. Many have just been moving. Some are going through social and emotional crises. Even under the best of circumstances they must make difficult adjustments. Often they are looking for help and that is why they come to church.
>
> New members require more pastoral care with greater intensity. The pastor has to get to know them. Where are their breaking points? What are their needs? They must have some kind of visit from a pastor.

The staff of the church coordinates new-member involvement. It gives high priority to the pastoral care of each new member. From their visits they learn what new folks are seeking. Every week the two pastors, the minister of music, and the part-time administrative assistant meet to plan the pastoral care for this important group. Name by name they discuss each visitor and each new member. What do they know about them? What have they learned in their visits or their contacts? Who needs another visit?

At each meeting of the session, pastors and elders go over that same list of visitors and new members. The staff interprets what they know about each one and shares what their needs are. If no one knows, they ask someone to find out. What have been their attendance patterns? What additional care do they need? Who best can give it?

THE IMPORTANCE OF LAY PASTORAL CARE

The wife of a retired minister underscores the opportunities that lay visitors have to minister to new people in a community. She worked first as a Welcome Wagon hostess and later in real estate sales. In these occupations she found many opportunities for ministry to new residents. Sensing that she was a caring person, and probably because she was a stranger, they would pour out their hearts to her. They had left their friends. The movers had broken things. They would discuss an amazing variety of intimate problems that they might not share with someone with whom they expected to have a long-term relationship.

In some ways she felt her opportunities for ministry were greater than a pastor would have. People often have a certain reserve with a minister whose visiting may aim to recruit them as members of the church. Lay pastoral care plays a critical role in the retention of church members, as the next chapter will show.

QUESTIONS FOR STUDY AND DISCUSSION

1. In what specific ways does your congregation welcome visitors? If you have greeters, what are their duties, and how are they trained? In what ways do you make certain that someone introduces visitors to members following the service or during your coffee hour? In what ways do you follow up with visitors? What suggestions do you have for ways to improve your welcome to visitors?

2. How do you prepare visitors for membership? Do you require them to take an inquirer's class? If not, why not? If so, do you take enough time to cover the subjects that need to be dealt with? How might you improve the way you prepare and receive new members?

3. Does your congregation hold high expectations for its members? If not, why not? If so, what are those expectations and how are they communicated to new members? What do your answers suggest for any changes the congregation might make?

4. What is the glue that holds your membership together? Does it in any way make it difficult for new members to be accepted to the inner circle of your church life? If so, what can you do about it?

5. In what ways does your congregation try to incorporate new members fully into the life of the church? Do you give them special pastoral attention as this chapter suggests? How do you involve them in the decision-making process of the church? Do you feel that new members experience psychological success as a result of their church involvement? What suggestions grow out of your answers to these questions?

RESOURCES

Oswald, Roy M., and Speed B. Leas. *The Inviting Church: A Study of New Member Assimilation,* Washington, D.C.: The Alban Institute, 1990.

Schaller, Lyle E. *Assimilating New Members.* Nashville: Abingdon Press, 1978.

7

EQUIP AND SUSTAIN
LAY SHEPHERDS

"We didn't leave the church, the church left us," said the couple whose son had been killed. "No one really seemed to care."

What can we do about inactive members?" congregations ask. "How do we keep them from dropping out?" So far we have avoided a direct answer. First, we wanted to make another point. A church that meets its members' needs for community, meaning, service, and belonging will keep most of them from drifting away. However, in any congregation members do become inactive and drop out. We must face that problem squarely. What can be done about it? Fortunately, there are exciting answers to that nagging question.

WHY MEMBERS DROP OUT

John Savage and his colleagues interviewed dropouts. They found that many felt no one had missed them or cared enough to find out why they were hurting. A third of them had such strong unresolved feelings that they cried during the interview. In his videotape *Drop Out Tracks,* Savage describes the steps through which dropouts go:

1. An "anxiety-provoking event" or cluster of events, such as some personal tragedy, burnout, or a conflict with the pastor, with another family in the church, or with members of their own family.

2. A verbal cry for help that the trained ear can hear.

3. Anger if no one responds to the cry for help.

4. Either a feeling of *helplessness* (blaming others for not doing something) or *hopelessness* (blaming one's self for not being able to do anything about the situation).

5. Withdrawal through a series of moves—from worship, from attending committee meetings, from Sunday school, taking children out of Sunday school, a letter of resignation, and no pledge.

6. Sealing off the pain and reinvestment in other activities if no response comes within six to eight weeks after a decision to leave the church.[1]

The sooner someone recognizes the cry for help and deals with it, the greater the chance of restoring an alienated member and the easier that restoration will be. However, those who respond to a cry for help must recognize that the presenting issues will not necessarily be the same as the sources of the person's deep underlying pain. And it is that pain they must deal with before resolution of the anxiety is possible. Congregations will be more likely to keep their members if they follow up on absent members quickly and consistently, if they recognize the cries for help and deal with them promptly and skillfully.

MOST INACTIVE-MEMBER PROGRAMS DON'T WORK

Most programs for dealing with inactive members are not effective. Seventy-five percent of churches in a United Presbyterian study had such programs; most were not successful. The General Assembly has urged churches to develop "more conscientious programs for the retention of members who become inactive or move away."[2]

Three out of five churches in our study have procedures for dealing with inactive members. Contrary to our expectations, however, high-loss churches were more likely than bonding churches to have such programs. One explanation is that most such programs are not successful. Of all congregations that have programs for inactive members, only six to seven percent rate them as "very effective." More than half do not believe they are even "somewhat effective."

So, what approaches to inactive members really work? Through telephone interviews and on-site visits, churches with effective programs gave us the answer.

TRAINED VISITORS MAKE THE DIFFERENCE

Where there are programs to reach inactive members, bonding churches are more than twice as likely as high-loss churches to use a core of callers trained to recognize cries for help and discover individuals' special needs. Half the small bonding churches with such programs used a core of trained callers compared with only 20 percent of small high-loss churches. Since many small churches are not concerned with procedures, that is a significant finding.

Visitation of all regular members does seem to make a difference. Bonding churches are far more likely than high-loss churches to be "very satisfied" with regular member visitation programs. Our follow-up interviews confirmed that two things enhance member loyalty: an effective visitation program for all members, and an inactive member program that makes use of well-trained callers.

PATIENCE, NOT PURGING

We found an intriguing policy difference between the two groups. Bonding churches are more likely than high-loss churches to say it is their policy to retain inactive members on the active roll in the hope that they will become active. Not surprisingly, this policy difference between small bonding churches and small high-loss churches is even greater.

If this policy is no more than a vague hope that members will become active without any accompanying action, we would say that the bonding churches simply have a higher proportion of sessions that are lax in clearing their membership rolls. While this was true for some churches in our study, further analysis of our data suggests that this does not fully explain the difference.

Many bonding churches appear to have a *redemptive* policy of membership conservation. They keep trying to minister to the needs of inactive members and thus win them back to participation in the life of the church. Meanwhile the names stay on their rolls. Their concern for young members who are away illustrates this. Bonding churches are more likely than high-loss churches to have programs that maintain active contact with absent college students or other young adults. They also are more likely to reestablish contact with young adults and students when they return during vacations and holidays.

The pastor of Good Shepherd Church is among the most dedicated and systematic callers of all pastors we interviewed. With some passion, he shared his philosophy. "We need less purging and more patience," he said. "Most sessions are too quick to take members off their rolls when they are inactive. Rather, it is our responsibility to work diligently to bring back those who are absenting themselves. Only when all else fails do we remove their names."

He told of an inactive family he had visited twice a year. When trouble came to them, he was there. Now they are active again. Another inactive member came back only after six years of regular visitation. That man is now an active deacon.

Whether all would agree with that amount of patience, the pastor's point is clear. It suggests a strategy for dealing with hard-core inactive members. They deserve particularly patient and persistent pastoral care. It should aim more to meet their needs and less to get them back in the pew.

SKILLED LAY PASTORAL CARE

Fortunately there are practical programs for training selected laity to give skilled pastoral care to members in crisis and to minister competently to inactive members.

L.E.A.D. CONSULTANTS WORKSHOPS, developed by John S. Savage. Lab I of Calling and Caring Ministries is a thirty-eight-hour training program. It gives participants basic skills to visit inactive members. Lab II is a fifty-hour event designed to train persons to lead Lab I.

STEPHEN MINISTRIES. The Stephen Series was developed by Kenneth G. Haugk, author of *Christian Caregiving—A Way of Life*. It trains and organizes laity for ministry to persons in crisis situations. Leaders attend a twelve-day training course and return to train and supervise volunteer Stephen ministers.

SHEPHERD PLANS. Churches divide their members into small groups with a deacon or some other caregiver responsible for each "fold" or zone. Both bonding and high-loss churches that have programs to keep in touch with their members mention shepherd programs more frequently than any other program. Unfortunately their effectiveness varies greatly. The secret of a good program seems to lie in careful selection of the shepherds and in their training and supervision. Geographical zones do not appear to be the best form of organization because they do not take into account existing personal relationships.

BOARD OF DEACONS. The office of deacon in the Presbyterian Church exercises ministries of caring on behalf of the congregation. Bonding churches have organized these functions in different ways. Often groups with specialized skills supplement the work of deacons and are responsible to them.

CALLING AND CARING LABS

The two-hundred-member Old Town Church is in a relatively stable old community in the eastern United States, yet it has been growing in membership. The pastor attributes much of this to the training members have received in active listening skills. After completing training in the L.E.A.D. program's Lab I and Lab II in calling and caring skills, she trained twenty members of her congregation.

Initially, the core of trained callers met monthly for supervision, mutual support, and planning of their visits. "It takes many visits to discover and deal with the deep causes of pain that keep members away," the pastor says.

> But they do come back. It does work. And when members come back, they often bring with them unchurched friends. For the first time, someone has heard their cries for help. Someone has cared enough to listen to their pain and anger. In fact, this program is a gold mine for new members! And we have had practically no loss of members at all.

In the past two years the calling group has not met together regularly, but they continue to hear the cries of pain. They minister to those who are hurting and alert the pastor to those who need her special skills. "People don't lose the listening skills they have learned," she observes.

Recently the congregation sponsored a weekend "Couples' Connection" aimed at enhancing the listening skills of marital partners. Twenty people participated, of whom twelve came from other churches. Not only did it heighten marital communication, it also sharpened listening skills of church leaders who participated.

The pastor now hopes to start a listening skills workshop for greeters. "People are most likely to make snide comments about the church when they enter the foyer," she asserts. Without training, a greeter is likely to miss the implication of such remarks or not know how to handle them. Trained greeters can pursue the deeper sources of dissatisfaction.

STEPHEN MINISTRY

Literally thousands of churches of many denominations participate in the Stephen Ministry program. Trained leaders select lay people with gifts of caring. They equip them with fifty hours training and commission them as Stephen ministers. The leaders give two hours of supervision a week and provide for continuing education.

Stephen ministers supplement the pastoral ministries of the professional staff. Each is paired with a care receiver. Their special ministry is to give extended care to members in crisis situations such as hospitalization, dying, divorce, grief, family crises, abuse, and rape. They listen, understand, and refer people for appropriate help. A twelve-year-old boy learns to express his anger at his parents' divorce. A Stephen minister guides a brain-damaged young man to a rehabilitation program. Parents of a man with an emotional problem also need help. The pastor assigns a Stephen minister to work with each of them.

Like some other bonding churches, Suburban First Church adapted the Stephen training program for its own use. It used *Christian Care Giving—A Way of Life* as a text, followed its *Leader's Guide,* and supplemented them with other materials. Leaders brought in a doctor, a nursing-home worker, a specialist in alcohol and drug abuse, a woman who had recovered from depression, and parents who were grieving over their young son who was killed in an accident. Experienced Stephen ministers met with the class periodically. When the program began, the pastor introduced it with a series of sermons on care-giving in the Bible.

An Effective Lay Shepherds Program

A seven-hundred-member congregation in the Northeast has an effective shepherding program. This may be one reason they have an average fall worship attendance of four hundred. They have divided members into thirty-two folds with five to seven families in each fold. Instead of a geographical distribution, shepherds themselves propose members of each fold.

Shepherds have four tasks: to pray every day for their fold, to be available to them, to contact them at least once a month, and to set an example of Christ's love. They build relationships with their flock to prepare for a time when they may need to give special help to some member.[3]

There are two workshops a year, one for beginners and one for advanced training. Upon completion of their training, shepherds are commissioned at a Sunday morning service. After that they meet quarterly.

Deacons do follow-up work in meeting the physical needs of members. They provide meals, transportation, and relief, for example, but shepherds provide the ongoing pastoral care.

There are forty-one lay shepherds, eighteen of whom have had extensive training in listening skills and in lay pastoral ministry. Six elders serve as shepherds to the shepherds, and the senior minister is the shepherd to the elders. A volunteer, also an elder, gives about twenty hours a week to coordinate the program. She has four assistants. One does the paper work to coordinate the calling. One does the computer work and sets up the folds.

One interviews potential shepherds. And one serves as a liaison with the board of deacons.

A large program such as this requires careful oversight. The enthusiastic and committed coordinator is the key to its success. How did she get involved? Several years ago, suffering from burnout, she was about to become inactive. When the presbytery offered Lab I training, her pastor suggested her name. She responded positively to the invitation and to the training. So she took Lab II and other postlab training and began the shepherd program in her congregation.

INACTIVE-MEMBER PROGRAMS THAT WORK

Broadview Church reviews its attendance records each month. For many years a volunteer has been following up with telephone calls to anyone who has been absent for four Sundays. She calls at dinner time to be sure they are home. "We have been missing you at church," she says. "I just called to see if you are all right." She makes a list for the pastor of anything she learns. One of the ministers follows up on any needs that require a pastoral call.

For many years Westminster Church has had a well-trained pastoral care team. It was established to help the pastor by calling on shut-ins and on members in hospitals and nursing homes. Now its efforts have been redirected to working with inactives.

The congregation is small enough that the pastor and the team usually know who is absent on Sunday morning. However, to keep a cumulative record, they ask members to fill out pew pads. Every other month the pastoral care team meets for training and to go over the list of absentees. They decide what friend or other natural contact would be the right person to make a visit. In the first contact they let people know they are missed. They may invite the absentee back to some area of prior interest, such as the bowling team. If the absentee *does* come back, they try to make reentry easy by being careful to "make no judgments and to ask no dumb questions." If a second contact is necessary, they seek to discover if something has happened that keeps the member from coming back.

A church of 325 members has an average Sunday worship attendance of well over half its members. A session committee on commitment together with six or eight volunteer visitors meets with the pastor once a month for training. This includes role playing and discussions on the purpose of their calls. They visit inactive members and those who come to worship very infrequently. Their task is *not* to get inactive members back in church. Rather, the visits have two foci: to share things that are happening in the immediate future such as a communion Sunday or a major event in the life of the church, and to explore the unmet needs of the members and discover how they are feeling about the church. In all they do, they are asking the question, "How can we be more helpful to you personally?"

A COMPREHENSIVE APPROACH TO LAY PASTORAL CARE

Covenant Church had a zone plan covering all seven hundred members of the church. Each of twenty-seven deacons had responsibility for care of from fifteen to twenty households. As with many such plans, other demands on the deacons preempted their doing much calling. Levels of care were inconsistent.

To create more manageable assignments and provide more consistent care, the church reorganized the board of deacons. It reallocated its functions and expanded the number of members from outside the board who would provide caregiving functions. A smaller board of eighteen deacons has become an administrative body with six committees, each of which coordinates an area of ministry. Each committee plans, oversees, and reviews the ministry for which it is responsible. Each recruits, supports, and supervises volunteers who carry out that ministry.

THE SHEPHERDS MINISTRY consists of two types of shepherd. A group shepherd is chosen from each organization in the church (Mariners, women's circles, Bible classes, choirs, etc.). Twenty-two such groups involve about half the members of the congregation. Twenty neighborhood shepherds are each responsible for eight to ten households whose members do not belong to any organization.

All shepherds are trained in how to visit members of their flock and how to keep track of their participation. Every three months they receive a list of families in their group or zone, showing worship attendance patterns for the previous quarter. They then are to make contact with any who have not been active and are to report within a week on what they have learned. Between these quarterly contacts, shepherds report any needs they discover.

Meanwhile, each week a church secretary records responses to the friendship pads. The associate pastor receives a list of those who have been absent for three to six weeks. Based on personal knowledge, he drops those whose situation does not require a pastoral visit. He then confers with the rest of the staff to determine what needs to be done for the others. Finally he telephones or visits those that require his attention. This pattern, in a large congregation, appears to have been very effective in dealing with inactive members at an early stage of their absence from worship.

THE HOMEBOUND MINISTRY assigns one homebound individual to each of thirty-five volunteers. Visitors call at least once a month. They offer the various resources of the church, including worship tapes, cassette players, home communion, pastoral visits, or other special support.

THE GOOD NEIGHBOR MINISTRY coordinates the delivery of food baskets to needy families at Christmas time and provides food for emergency needs. It recommends use of the deacons' fund to support community agencies that meet emergency needs of individuals and families.

THE TRANSPORTATION MINISTRY coordinates drivers for the van on Sunday mornings and for other church transportation needs.

THE PRAYER CHAIN MINISTRY transmits prayer requests to deacons and others on the prayer chain. One deacon coordinates this.

THE BLOODMOBILE MINISTRY coordinates regular blood drives in cooperation with the American Red Cross.
    Complementing the work of the deacons is the Stephen Ministry, which provides crisis care. The associate pastor assigns members to Stephen ministers as needs become apparent.

JUDICATORY RESOURCING

Old Town Church is part of a presbytery that provides Lab I training to members of its churches twice a year. Ten ministers and lay trainers have completed the Lab II program, and about three hundred members of different churches have completed the Lab I program.
    This is just one of the continuing education and leadership development programs that the Presbytery Academy offers. Its half-time director also serves as pastor of a hundred-member church. The Academy recruits people for Lab I training in four ways. (1) Its six-hour Saturday training program for deacons gives a two-and-a-half-hour introduction to listening skills. (2) The Academy director encourages participants to take the six-hour course on crisis visitation, including ministry to the sick and the dying. (3) In forty-five-minute presentations to sessions, the academy director outlines John Savage's *Drop Out Tracks*. (4) He then offers a three-hour course on listening skills to elders. These various courses have enrollments of from twenty to thirty people. Out

of those different introductory experiences come people who are willing to commit thirty-eight hours to the Lab I program.

"The problem we have," says the academy director,

> is getting the program going beyond participation in Lab I. If a pastor and session do not commit themselves to developing a listening ministry, the program in a congregation will die within a year. However, if the program has their support, and if a minimum of eight to ten members have taken Lab I, the program can be successful. The ideal in any congregation is to train 10 percent of the members. This will almost slam the back door to membership loss.

The numbers are important because callers need a support group. They get together to share their experiences and to receive further training. Four congregations in the presbytery are successfully operating the program.

The academy director says that Savage research has concluded that a program with highly trained listeners can expect to bring back 46 percent of members who have dropped out for one year. Nearly a quarter of those who have dropped out for five years or more will probably return. If the program focuses on early visits to members whose cries of pain have been heard, one can expect a 98 percent retention rate.

One of the principal obstacles to the program in this particular presbytery is its cultural context. There is a strong family orientation, and people are very conservative. Change is not easy to accept. Many of the small churches are in coal-mining communities where family fatalities from mining accidents have been endemic. People do not readily deal with their feelings and tend to store up their hurts. As a result, many families are basically dysfunctional. One does not wash dirty linen in public. Thus one does not go to someone for help because that is a sign that something is wrong.

OTHER RESOURCES

CARING FOR INACTIVE MEMBERS: HOW TO MAKE GOD'S HOUSE A HOME is a new curriculum developed by Kenneth Haugk out of his experience with the Stephen Series. It contains a text, a participant manual, and a leader's guide. This material has been developed so recently that we did not find it in use in any of the bonding churches.

THE INTERNATIONAL LAY PASTORS MINISTRY NETWORK is an organization for pastors, staff, and lay people who are leading a lay pastoral care ministry or who want to learn how to start or restart one. Melvin Steinbron is its coordinator.

QUESTIONS FOR STUDY AND DISCUSSION

1. What program(s) do you have for the ongoing pastoral care of your members? Calling by the pastor or staff members? Lay pastoral calling by Stephen ministers? A shepherd or zone plan? How effective do you judge the program(s) to be? What suggestions might you make as a result of your discussion of this chapter?

2. How do you react to the policy of some congregations that favors patience not purging of inactive members? Is this just an excuse for not taking the unpleasant action of clearing your rolls? What redemptive action might your congregation take in dealing with inactive members?

3. In what ways does your congregation work with its inactive members? How effective is that approach? Do you keep track of members who are absent? How soon do you follow up in contacting them? Does a core of trained callers visit them? What suggestions would you make for a more effective approach?

RESOURCES

Haugk, Kenneth G. *Caring for Inactive Members: How to Make God's House a Home*. St Louis: Tebunah Ministries, 1990. Leader's guide and participant's manual. Tebunah Ministries, 7053 Lindell Boulevard, St. Louis, MO 63130.

————. *Christian Caregiving—A Way of Life*. Minneapolis: Augsburg Publishing House, 1984.

Haugk, Kenneth G., and William J. McKay. *Christian Caregiving—A Way of Life, Leader's Guide*. Minneapolis: Augsburg Publishing House, 1986.

International Lay Pastors Ministry Network, 7132 Portland Avenue, Minneapolis, MN 55423.

L.E.A.D. Consultants, Inc., P.O. Box 664, Reynoldsburg, OH 43068. (614) 864-0156. Lab I and Lab II, calling and caring ministries.

Savage, John S. *The Apathetic and Bored Church Member: Psychological and Theological Implications*. Reynoldsburg, Ohio: L.E.A.D. Consultants, Inc., 1976.

————. *Drop Out Tracks.* Reynoldsburg, Ohio: L.E.A.D. Consultants, Inc., 1987. Videotape.

Steinbron, Melvin J. *Can the Pastor Do It Alone?* Ventura, Calif.: Regal Books, 1987.

Stephen Ministries, 1325 Boland, St. Louis, MO 63117. (314)645-5511.

8

CHANNEL CONFLICTS CREATIVELY

You have called us from division
Into unity and hope.
Each and all belong together
In the world's kaleidoscope.
Help us listen to the voices
Daring us to be and do
What you plan for church and people,
Loving others, praising you.

JANE PARKER HUBER[1]

The most startling discovery in our study was the amount of destructive conflict that exists in Presbyterian churches. Out of 439 churches who responded to questions about conflict, 53 percent have experienced serious conflicts at some time during the past five years. This includes 65 percent of high loss churches and 43 percent of bonding churches.

One-third of the high-loss churches that have experienced conflict lost members as a result of their conflict. Of the pastors involved, 35 percent left their pastorates. One-fifth of bonding churches lost members, and 19 percent of their pastors left. Without comparable statistics from other denominations, we can only note the plethora of books on conflict management and assume that conflict is a serious problem for them as well.

Conflicts in any organization are inevitable. And, of course, not all conflicts are destructive. They can be a source of energy and creativity. They can strengthen a congregation if managed properly. They can be devastating if they are not. Indeed, the way in which a congregation deals with conflict can make or break it.

CAUSES OF CONFLICT

Out of churches in our study that had experienced serious conflict, 58 percent named pastoral leadership and interpersonal differences between pastors and members as a cause. Two-thirds of the high-loss churches and roughly half the bonding churches mentioned these causes.

Interpersonal differences between members was the second most frequent cause and occurred 31 percent of the time. One quarter of the churches identified other causes as well. In order of frequency, their disagreements were over finances, policies or practices, programs, theology or values, and worship style.[2]

DOES INVOLVEMENT IN SOCIAL ACTION CAUSE CONFLICT?

There is a widespread myth that involvement in social action is a major cause of membership loss. Research efforts have failed to establish this. We found that only 9 percent of churches that had experienced serious conflict attributed it to disagreement over a social-action emphasis. This compares with 6 percent that identified an emphasis on evangelism as the cause of conflict.

SHATTERED EXPECTATIONS CAUSE CONFLICTS

The unintentional silent treachery of shattered expectations can shipwreck the best of relationships. Our dreams for those relationships lie hidden to our consciousness until they die when we least expect it. Suddenly our disappointments pile up, and we find ourselves in deep disagreement. Broken expectations can lead to fight or flight, or to apathy and drift.

Every member has expectations of the pastor and of the church. However, few are aware of them. Images of pastors and churches they have liked or disliked are shrouded in the mists of deeply hidden memories. All pastors have expectations of congregations that have wooed them. When conflicts arise, it is often because neither pastor nor people have ever expressed their expectations.

All of us need dependable relationships. Fulfilled expectations are the basis of trust and of bonding. Clarified expectations improve the chances of their fulfillment and of developing dependable relationships. Implicit or ambiguous expectations may prove to be time bombs. One never knows when one of them will emerge with explosive force and destroy relationships of trust.

An important antidote to destructive conflict is the sharing of mutual expectations at the beginning of a relationship. At that time it is essential to set up a mechanism for reviewing and revising those expectations.

PINCH HEARERS

In his Lab I program, John Savage describes a role negotiation model developed by John Sherwood.[3] It outlines four stages in the maintenance of a long-term relationship:

Developing role clarity by exchanging information on mutual expectations.

Making a commitment to the way in which people in the relationship will relate to one another.

Productivity and stability in the relationship. This results from role clarity.

Disruption of expectations when expectations are violated.

In this model a pinch is one's reaction to a violation of an expectation. A pinch may result from omission or commission. A continuing healthy relationship must provide for open communication between the parties involved whenever there is a pinch. If this does not happen, pinches pile up. These lead to a crunch point that disrupts the relationship. When a pinch occurs, a planned renegotiation of the expectations needs to follow.

We have already suggested that new-member classes should clarify mutual expectations. Pastor and people agree to come to each other when any of them experiences a pinch in their relationship.

A congregation of five hundred members developed a "pinch hearer" program based on this model. In their new-member orientation program, the pastor describes the conflict resolution model in detail. He predicts that members will surely get pinched at some time or other. He asks them to commit themselves to call him or a trained pinch hearer when that happens.

The congregation has trained sixty pinch hearers in Lab I listening skills. Many also have had Stephen Ministry training. Five pinch hearers are on active duty each quarter. The bulletin lists their names and telephone numbers. It reminds members that broken expectations are inevitable and asks them to use a pinch hearer when that happens.

This approach will work in a congregation of any size. Train a few pinch hearers. Explain the model to all members and ask them to use it.

CLERGY IN THE CROSS FIRE

Conflict can erupt whenever a pastor's unexpressed self-expectations for ministry differ from the unarticulated and differing expectations of members in the pew or in the governing body with which the pastor works.

Pastors and churches can reduce this role conflict and ambiguity in the pastoral ministry by (1) clarifying mutual expectations at the beginning of the pastorate, (2) negotiating a description of the pastor's responsibilities in relationship to the responsibilities of that body, (3) agreeing on patterns of communication that will keep the expectations alive and flexible, (4) using interrelated goal setting for the congregation and the pastor, (5) agreeing on a process for reviewing the performance of each, and (6) providing for periodic renegotiation of mutual expectations and of the pastor's responsibility description.[4]

Clergy in the Cross Fire[5] gives pastors the following additional clues for reducing role conflicts and ambiguity:

CLARIFY THE CONGRUENCE of your goals with those of the church. What is the mission of the congregation, and what are its goals? To what extent do your expectations contribute toward those goals? If not, how can you reconcile them?

KNOW YOURSELF. To reduce ambiguity in the expectations of others, pastors must understand their own strengths and weaknesses. They need to be clear about their own understanding of the church and of ministry and about their own goals. They must know the roles they can play most effectively. Then they need to communicate this to all concerned and encourage others to play roles that supplement their weaknesses.

CHECK YOUR PERCEPTIONS. Do you really know what others expect of you? The results of several studies suggest that ministers do not accurately assess the feelings of their people about their work. So they need feedback from others they can trust.

DO NOT RUN AWAY. Under concerted role conflict, ministers tend to withdraw psychologically. This tendency is more pronounced when pastors feel that others question the quality of their performance. But withdrawal is a self-defeating mechanism. It only increases ambiguity or conflict. Instead, increase your communication with others involved.

DISCUSS YOUR ROLE with your board and let them interpret it to the congregation. There is evidence that discussion of the minister's role by clergy and laity increases consensus among all concerned.

STUDY THE DYNAMICS of those who expect things of you. How deeply involved are they in those expectations? How powerful are they in enforcing them? How observable to them are the role conflicts? How legitimate are the different claims they make on you?

WHEN OTHERS DISAGREE among themselves on what they expect of you, let it be their problem, not yours. As they struggle to resolve their differences, they may better realize the bind they have been putting you in.

WHEN YOU ARE IN A BIND, do not be passive. Actively renegotiate your roles. In so far as possible, do so in such a way that the needs of everyone are met.

WORK CLOSELY with a personnel committee whose members you can trust. They need to support you but also to challenge you when you need challenging. When the emperor wears no clothes, someone had better tell him.

BE BIG ENOUGH to call in an outside consultant when the situation requires it. A lay leader who operates a presbytery-sponsored mediation service finds that ministers often do not call for mediation when they need it. "Their attitude seems to be, 'If I can't handle it, neither can you.' "

CONGREGATIONAL CORPORATE PAIN

When a pastor and a congregation are in conflict, it is sometimes difficult to discern whether the pastor or the congregation is causing the conflict. There are some churches, however, that grind up one pastor after another. They are in endless conflict.

John S. Savage observes that graduates of the L.E.A.D. Lab programs who go back to congregations in certain settings have outstanding results. As many as 40 percent to 60 percent of dropouts are restored to the active life of the congregation. In other congregations, however, graduates with identical training effect only a small return. Out of this, he has identified the concept of corporate pain. "Congregations that build corporate pain delete their resourceful people," says Savage. "They are incapable of incorporating inactive members who are in pain because they, as a congregation, have not dealt with their own corporate pain."[6] There are various possible causes of corporate pain:

A pastoral leadership style that is demeaning or belittling of others.

Times of trauma in the life of the congregation that are not worked through but denied.

Rapid turn-over of pastoral leadership that causes congregations to blame the system for their troubles.

The symptoms of corporate pain include

Very low energy. The more a congregation denies its traumatic events, the more energy they use to suppress them. A symptomatic response from a pastor may be "I can't get my congregation to do anything."

Excessive or inappropriate pious language used as a denial or a screening of pain.

"Regular bonfires of controversy."[7] The pastor becomes exhausted from trying to extinguish one conflict after another.

Scapegoating. The congregation focuses its pain on a vulnerable person. Often it is the pastor, but it can be a lay person. If the pastor tries to deal with this by preaching a sermon, he simply fires up the pain and a "conflict loop" develops.

L.E.A.D.'s five-day workshop titled "Congregational Corporate Pain" deals with various forms of conflict and the resolution of such pain. "When you have uncorked the corporate pain," says Savage, "you can turn pain into creative energy for the development of long range goals and mission."[8]

JOE BROWN'S CONFLICT MANAGEMENT STYLE

In Chapter 5 we saw how Joe Brown's intimate involvement in a small community and his caring ministry in a hundred-member church enabled him to lead his congregation into facing controversial issues without destructive conflict.
Of his conflict management style, Joe Brown says,

I am not afraid of conflict. I am open and honest about disagreements. I am confrontive in dealing with differences. I don't hide them.

People know where I stand on issues. I don't expect people to agree with me. They listen to me, and I listen to them. But disagreements never keep me from ministering to the needs of the people. If you don't do your caring, if you don't demonstrate the love of God and emphasize your oneness in Christ, conflicts will get you kicked out. You won't be able to stand the pain.

"Because of some of the stances I have taken," he goes on to explain, "some members have left the church. But more have come in than have left. Some in the community have ridiculed me. They have even called me a 'communist.' But the people of our congregation defend me and my right to express those judgments."

One evening as the meeting of session was about to begin, four of the six elders turned to Pastor Brown. "Two of us," they said, "are so angry they are not speaking to each other. We've got to resolve the problem before we can proceed with the meeting."

"And so," says Pastor Brown, "we listened to a lot of hurt and let them know that all of us cared. But we did not try to tell them what to do. Later I also met with them individually. They found a way to resolve their differences. Today, the two of them work together as team leaders of our youth group."

How does this pastor deal with the stress in his own life that conflict produces?

I have a wonderful wife. I have a marvelous personnel committee that works with me closely. I have taken a continuing education course on stress management. And one of the greatest things I did when I began my ministry here was to set up an informal support group. I chose two or three people I can call to talk things over. They are great prayer partners. So I have a couple of members I lean on when I need support.

Another thing that helps is that I am here by choice. There have been several opportunities for me to move. I have declined. I know that I could move if I wanted to. And the people know it too. This gives me a freedom in dealing with difficult situations I would not otherwise feel.

Once a year Joe Brown's theme for the sermon and for the service is repentance and forgiveness. He prays for forgiveness for any time during the year when he may have hurt anyone either intentionally or unintentionally.

PROACTIVE PEACEMAKING

Bonding pastors manage conflicts promptly and use them as opportunities for members to grow. John Jones is pastor of an inner-city congregation of a hundred members in a blue-collar neighborhood. He preaches and teaches peacemaking, not only globally but in individual lives. Repeatedly he makes clear that he is accessible to help people work through their disagreements. They often come to him about ways in which other members have hurt their feelings or otherwise are in conflict with them. Because the congregation is small, he knows everyone and notices when they are not in Sunday worship. If someone has been inactive for several weeks, he calls them.

The church is very active in serving the neighborhood. So members have a good deal of interaction with each other. They usually say what they think. They know where others are coming from, but some do get hurt in the process.

Jones faces problems squarely and deals with conflicts promptly. "I don't let them simmer," he says. "It's just my nature to help people solve their differences without demeaning them." Within a day or two he talks with the persons involved either face-to-face or on the telephone. Just before our interview, he had called a member who had absented herself from worship for two weeks. He discovered that a conflict with their part-time student minister had hurt her feelings. During the past two years Pastor Jones has been instrumental in helping members work through their differences at least ten times.

Fellowship Church has had its conflict experiences too. How have they handled them? Members deal with disagreements by keeping open communication: "We try to help each other see another point of view. People here really can accept and love others where they are. So we feel safe to say negative things." The three previous pastors have been good listeners. They have known how to compromise and have not taken sides but have worked to hold the congregation together. When conflict has involved the minister himself, "adept people on the session have smoothed the way. They have talked with the pastor and convinced him of what needed to be done."

We found in our study that key members of bonding churches are more likely than key members of high-loss churches to agree strongly that their pastor develops a spirit of unity within the congregation.

DIFFERENT STYLES FOR MANAGING CONFLICT

There are many styles for managing conflict. Speed Leas of the Alban Institute conducts many conflict management seminars. He has developed an instrument called *Discover Your Conflict Management Style.*[9] Answering forty-five forced-choice questions helps people identify which of six styles of conflict management they tend to use. Leas then describes those six styles in detail. After each description he tells how and when to use that style and what the results of that approach are likely to be.

The styles he includes, along with some possible results, are

Persuasion. It is not likely to result in change unless there is a strong trust level and strong commitment to you.

Compelling or forcing. Compliance will occur only under direct supervision and morale will be low.

Avoiding/ignoring/accommodating/fleeing. This does not change anything, and persistent use leads to depressed organizations.

Collaboration. This generates high motivation to carry out joint decisions and increased quality of decisions.

Bargaining or negotiation. The results are similar to those from collaboration but with less commitment.

Support (active listening). Supported persons take responsibility for themselves, but some may wish you had taken sides with them.

COPING WITH CONFLICT

There are two excellent videos called *Coping with Conflict.*[10] A users' guide and a conflict intensity chart accompany them. The chart describes five levels of conflict, suggests skills needed to deal with them, and proposes appropriate response strategies. The levels, together with suggested response strategies, are:

Level One: Problem to solve (disagreement over conflicting goals, values, or needs). This requires skills that all members of a judicatory committee on ministry can learn.

Level Two: Disagreement (personalities and issues get mixed). This requires specialized training of carefully selected persons from the committee on ministry.

Level Three: Contest (win/lose dynamics are at work). This needs an experientially trained crisis intervention team.

Level Four: Fight/flight (a shift from winning to getting rid of people). This requires intervention by a consultant with considerable experience.

Level Five: Intractable (the conflict is unmanageable: the issue is lost, and personalities have become the issue). Plan to rebuild relationships, and support all members of the church.

A Conflict Resolution Group

In response to a request for help in a conflict situation involving pastor and congregation, one presbytery takes the following steps:

1. The committee on ministry appoints two teams. Each includes a pastor and an elder. One team serves as liaison and advocate for the pastor; the second as liaison and advocate for others involved in the conflict.

2. The two teams meet with the chairperson of the committee on ministry and the presbytery executive. This conflict resolution group works together throughout the process. They begin with a briefing on the situation.

3. Each team meets with and listens to its party to the conflict.

4. The two teams report to the conflict resolution group what they have heard. As far as possible, they advocate their party's position.

5. The conflict resolution group then seeks objectively to discover possible solutions to the conflict that they can propose to the pastor and others involved.

6. The two teams return to their parties and interpret what other parties to the conflict may be willing to do. They then propose the approach agreed upon by the conflict resolution group.

7. In some cases the congregation must act to accept the pastor's resignation, renegotiate the pastor's contract, or otherwise deal with the problem. In that event, the conflict resolution group interprets its findings to the congregation before it acts.

In more than one instance, this approach has reduced conflicts to a level that has avoided a rupture of relationships and the resignation of the pastor. In other instances the conflict has not been resolved. In that case, both sides to the conflict have still felt that the presbytery has been helpful in their dealings with each other.

In situations where conflicted positions have hardened, it may be necessary for them to be unfrozen before the two teams do their work. In those cases someone may need to prepare the way for them.

A Judicatory Mediation Service

In 1985 a presbytery peacemaking committee wanted to make peacemaking practical for members of their congregations. A professional mediator and arbitrator convinced them to establish a presbytery mediation service that offers mediation services without charge to church members and groups.

Thirty-four volunteer laypersons took a comprehensive course in mediation at a nearby law school. They work with everything from family disputes to merchant-consumer disagreements. They have also helped congregations deal with serious disagreements and developing factions.

In one church the Christian education committee was torn by conflict. A new chairperson of the committee radically changed the committee's style of operation. The committee had always done its business very informally and made decisions casually. The chairperson had a military background and conducted the business brusquely and with dispatch. Members were upset. Two quit the church.

After talking with the parties concerned, the mediator brought them together to discuss their differences. "We never realized you had a military background!" committee members said with surprise.

"I didn't know how you were used to conducting your business," she replied. Out of mediation came a change in her style of leadership and a restructuring of the committee's work. The session learned it should give new committee members more careful orientation.

In another church the preschool staff was in turmoil. The director asked for mediation and discovered there was need for better communication among the staff. She started a weekly staff bulletin, installed mail boxes, and sent frequent memos to staff members.

Mediators served a congregation where differences in theological perspective between Koreans born in the United States and those born in Korea eventually led to a separation. The value? Less antipathy among the members concerned.

In another congregation a few members who were concerned only for their own agenda and not for the larger good of the congregation proved too difficult for the pastor to handle. He needed training in conflict management, which the mediation service provided him. The members finally left, however, because the congregation was not ready to accept their particular agenda.

The professional mediator and arbitrator who has been a key in this program says that the words *conflict* and *mediation* are frightening to church members and especially to ministers. "The heart of our faith is reconciliation. However, they do not seem to recognize that this implies conflict and estrangement. To reach them we need to talk about *negotiation* and *problem solving* or *dealing with disagreements.*"

"Reconciliation," he observes, "is one tenet of our faith we ignore. In doing so we lose members. People come to church to deal with their dissatisfactions and unresolved conflicts. Some churches give them pat answers that suffice for a time. What we need to do is give them a process to resolve their problems within themselves and with others."

THE EXECUTIVE PRESBYTER AS THIRD-PARTY NEGOTIATOR

Serious conflict erupted between the session of a multiple-staff congregation and its pastor. The congregation had a history of calling pastors who did not fit the needs of that church. Their current pastor was also a misfit, even though he had been called after a lengthy search process. His style was authoritarian. There was serious conflict between him and members of his staff. Members of the session had tried to help him work through his problems. He could not hear what people were saying to him.

The situation grew worse, and the session called in a consultant in conflict management. Nothing seemed to help. As a last resort the members of the session asked the executive presbyter to help them. As a rule, he is very cautious about intervening unless asked to do so by a pastor or session. He agreed to work with them on condition that they would allow him to conduct a meeting of the session.

He convinced the session to create a personnel committee. The pastor was to appoint its members. This was to insure that he had an opportunity to have the ear of people he could trust. The personnel committee interviewed those involved. They tried to get the pastor to understand what was going on. He could not hear them. Finally they came to the conclusion that the pastor had to leave.

At a special meeting of the session the executive got elders to speak their piece, insisting that they take responsibility for what they said. It became clear that the pastor would have to go. So the executive negotiated with them a terminal package that would keep the pastor whole financially until he could receive a call from another congregation.

In the executive's mind the issues then were, first, how to get the pastor to leave without splitting the congregation; second, how to help the pastor grow through the experience so he could learn to listen and profitably accept another call more suitable to his gifts; and third, how to help the congregation develop a more realistic understanding of who they were and what kind of a pastor they ought to call.

Gently but firmly he confronted the pastor with the fact that his situation was no longer viable. He had to leave. "Your time is over," he insisted, "You need to accept that reality with grace and integrity." The session would recommend severance arrangements that would span this difficult transition period in his life. The presbytery would help him secure a therapist to give him the personal counsel he needed. It would enable him to go to a career center where he could get the vocational guidance he needed. After he had profited from those interventions, the executive would help him develop a dossier and secure a call.

While the pastor was getting the help he needed, the executive met with the congregation. More than a hundred members were present at the meeting. The executive felt it was imperative to break the behavioral cycle that led to the mismatches between the pastors they had called and the demands of their situation. He led them in a self-examination process in which they identified their congregational personality and outlined their implicit value system. They came to realize that in calling a series of pastors they had been operating on assumptions and perceptions that simply did not fit the reality of who they were.

With the advice of the executive presbyter, the committee on ministry of the presbytery helped the session find a skilled interim pastor. He was chosen for his ability to heal some of the hurt in the congregation and as a model for the kind of ministry they needed. In due time they set up a search committee and found a pastor who now is leading them in effective ministry. "They are going like gangbusters!" the executive exclaims with satisfaction. The pastor completed his counseling and received a fine call suited to his gifts.

The key ingredients in this situation were as follows:

A skilled executive presbyter who knew when and how to intervene and was able to confront session, pastor, and congregation, and to hold the session accountable for its actions.

A trust relationship between the committee on ministry and the executive presbyter. This enabled them to let him intervene on their behalf while keeping the chair of the committee informed every step of the way.

Provision by the presbytery of funds to help pay for the pastor's therapy and occupational counseling, plus help for the pastor in preparing a dossier that would make it possible for him to find a new call.

Examination with the session of flexible options that enabled them to put together a fair termination package.

Firm but compassionate dealing with the pastor so he could grow into a more effective servant of the Lord.

Help for the congregation in finding a skilled interim minister to carry them through the transition and to model the kind of ministry they needed.

In conclusion this executive reports, "Ninety-eight percent of the troubles in my experience are between the pastor and the session or between the pastor and staff. In almost every conflict I have found that sessions have been reasonable and have exercised patience in the midst of their frustration and anger."

QUESTIONS FOR STUDY AND DISCUSSION

1. How does your congregation clarify the expectations of new members? Does the pinch hearer plan have possibilities for use in your congregation? What would be its advantages and disadvantages?

2. How does your church clarify the congregation's expectations of the pastor and the pastor's expectations of the congregation? Does the pastor have a position description? Is it revised periodically? Do church officers and the pastor clarify their respective roles and use goal setting and performance review or other similar methods?

3. How does your congregation manage disagreements that arise between members? Between the pastor and staff? Between the pastor and church officers or other members? How might you improve the way you deal with disagreements?

4. What styles for managing conflict are most comfortable for those of you who are discussing this chapter? What styles are most comfortable for other members of your church? Would it help you to get a clearer understanding of the value of different possible styles?

5. If your congregation were to get involved in a serious conflict, which resources in your presbytery or district conference would you want to have available? A conflict resolution group? A judicatory mediation service? Third-party negotiation? What resources are available to you now?

RESOURCES

Toward Improvement of Ministry series. Church Vocations Ministry Unit. Presbyterian Church (U.S.A.). 100 Witherspoon Street, Louisville, KY 40202-1396. (502)569-5765.

Leas, Speed B. *A Lay Person's Guide to Conflict Management.* Washington D.C.: The Alban Institute, 1979. The Alban Institute, 4125 Nebraska Avenue NW, Washington, D.C. 20016. (800)242-5226.

————. *Discover Your Conflict Management Style.* Washington, D.C.: The Alban Institute, 1985.

————. *Leadership and Conflict.* Nashville: Abingdon Press, 1982.

————. *Moving Your Church Through Conflict.* Washington, D.C.: The Alban Institute, 1985.

Pneuman, Roy W., and Margaret E. Bruehl. *Managing Conflict: A Complete Process-Centered Handbook.* Englewood Cliffs, N.J.: Prentice-Hall, Inc., 1982.

Savage, John S. *Role Negotiation Model.* Reynoldsburg, Ohio: L.E.A.D. Consultants, Inc., 1987. Videotape.

Smith, Donald P. *Clergy in the Cross Fire: Coping with Role Conflicts in the Ministry.* Philadelphia: Westminster Press, 1973.

Synod of Lakes and Prairies, *Coping with Conflict.* 1988. Videotapes. Available from Church Vocations Ministry Unit, Presbyterian Church (U.S.A.), 100 Witherspoon Street, Louisville, KY 40202-1396. (502)569-5765.

9

NOURISH FAMILIES
AND SUPPORT SINGLES

Many baby boomers are coming back to church. Most are married with children; some are single parents. One finds them in congregations that meet the needs of families. Parents want their children to understand what faith is about and to have a good educational experience. If they do not find it, they leave. Quality family ministries not only attract new members, they keep them.

"I grew up in this church," one young man said.

When I went away to college, it was dying. The same people were just getting older. When I came back, it was alive! There was excitement in the air. There were young people, children, and members of all ages. They were loving one another and caring about each other. It was family-oriented. The difference was so obvious that it drew me closer into its life. I wouldn't be here today if not for that change.

What had happened in those few years? A new pastor had come with a vision of what Trinity Church might become. It would center its life in Jesus Christ. People of all ages would grow in their faith by learning what the Bible could mean to them in their daily lives. It would have a strong family-oriented program while making singles feel welcome, too. This vision has come to fruition. There is an active ministry to parents, and children, and members of all ages. In nine years the church has grown from 750 to twelve hundred members even though the city has not been growing.

Immanuel Church had a good program for its older members. When the new pastor arrived, he noticed a big gap. People in their thirties and forties were not there even though the church was in a community with many families. He convinced the church to emphasize a ministry to young families without lessening its appeal to older members. Most new members during the past decade have been young families. Now the church overflows with children and young people. To house this beehive of activity, they recently completed a young-family center. Meanwhile the neighborhood has remained static, but the church membership has increased from 1,550 to nearly eighteen hundred members.

Members of the much smaller Fellowship Church were growing old, and younger folks were not joining the church. Before calling a new minister, they surveyed their members. People responded that their greatest strength was their "good loving family feeling." Members wanted most to attract young families who were moving into the community. They called a young, energetic minister with a family. He shared their vision of a family-oriented church but knew they must not neglect their older or single members. Today young couples and children have joined the church in an exciting fulfillment of that congregation's dream. And they have grown to nearly three hundred members.

These three congregations have much in common in spite of their difference in size. Skillfully, their pastors have articulated their vision of what a focus on families can mean. They have convinced their congregations to commit needed resources to that dream. They have a gift for identifying strong lay leadership and enlisting them to make dreams come true. They have continued to meet the needs of older members. They are "everyone's pastor." So members have been willing to support the new emphasis.

All three selected dynamic staff members to direct their programs. Two had directors of Christian education who sparked countless creative ministries for children and youth. One was full-time; the other part-time. The third church has a part-time director of children's ministry and a youth minister.

All three have developed outstanding preschool programs, two of which include education in the faith. The largest church also has a toddler's learning center.

All three carefully selected a cadre of volunteer leaders. They recruited and trained them to develop and direct their youth club programs. All have enlisted parents and many other volunteers in conducting those programs.

Our study found that bonding churches are more likely than high-loss churches to have family, marriage, and parenting programs, church schools for children, church youth groups, children's choirs, and youth choirs. Small bonding churches are much more likely than small high-loss churches to have all these programs, except choirs for children and youth. More of their members are very satisfied with their church school for children. Those that have children's choirs are more satisfied with them.

CRIB CONNECTION

The *Effective Christian Education* study showed that Christian nurture by parents is key to the faith maturity of developing children. The "crib connection" encourages parents to begin this with their newborn infants.[1]

Every new baby in the congregation is assigned to a trained crib connector. She brings the mother attractive literature that gives guidance on nurturing children in the Christian faith. She offers the services of the crib room at the church, which is staffed by trained young people.

Every month for a year the crib connector mails a printed leaflet to the new mother. This describes the stage of development the child may have reached. It suggests ways parents can help the infant grow in faith. Crib connectors are encouraged to visit more than once. Some become such good friends that the family invites them to the child's baptism. They often tell the Christian education director of particular family needs to which the church can respond.

Initial training for crib connectors includes active listening and other modules from the Stephen Series. Four times a year they meet for further training and support. A coordinator recruits connectors and assigns the newborns. One church persuaded a grandmother who had lost her husband to start the program. She proved to be a good organizer, and the program took off. In another church the talented coordinator is a mother with a great love for children and empathy with parents.

Fellowship Church puts the names and pictures of newborn children on a bulletin board in the foyer of the church. Ocean View Church links a prayer partner with each newborn child during its first year of life.

PRESCHOOL

Several bonding churches have preschool programs. Some are private schools that use the church building. Most have some tie with the church. Some are semiautonomous and self-select their board from church members. Others have advisory boards responsible to the session. Most churches see their preschool as a mission outreach into the community. Some include Christian instruction in the curriculum. Others do not. They tend to have strong feelings about their differing policies on that.

At Trinity Church, one of the pastor's early dreams was to have a preschool with a clearly Christian emphasis along with the best of developmental approaches. Little children and their parents need quiet but specific nurturing in their faith without oppressive or smothering religious pressure. He convinced the session that the church should do more than rent its space to a quality community-oriented preschool program. Here was an opportunity for a Christian ministry to families in and outside the church. He promised that within five years the school would be financially self-sustaining except for its use of space. His prediction has come true.

Before enrolling their children, parents receive a booklet that explains the school's goals for the social, conceptual, and motor development of their children. They learn that in the area of spiritual development the school's goals for each child are

to develop an appreciation of and response to God's love for them,

to experience prayer as talking with God,

to have a growing faith in Jesus as Lord and Savior, experiencing that faith on their individual development level.

Monthly goals for spiritual growth relate to the seasons and to special holidays. At a monthly chapel one of the ministers tells a story. At Christmas, the children put on a program in the sanctuary. In May they sing at one Sunday worship service.

A year after its founding the preschool took in some handicapped children, tuition free, as a mission project. Teachers feel that their presence helps in the development of all the children.

Almost every new-member class includes parents attracted to the church by its preschool or nursery programs. "We had fallen away from the church," one active member told us. "When we moved here, I brought my two-year-old daughter here because I had heard about the nursery."

To raise money for preschool equipment and supplies, the church holds an annual strawberry festival. Church women pick the strawberries and contribute food. There are activities for preschool children such as pony rides, a train ride, a clown face, and dunking. As many as four thousand people from all over town participate. The traffic congestion is so great that the church has to hire extra police. In addition to the ten thousand dollars raised, the strawberry festival helps people in the community see the church as human. What started as a fund-raiser has become a community event.

YOUTH CLUB

One of the most dynamic ministries to children is youth club. "Logos" is a midweek program for children and young people from kindergarten through senior high school. We judged its appeal to be greatest with elementary children. One day each week after school, children come to church for Bible study, crafts, choirs, recreation, and dinner. One of the youth choirs sings at the Sunday worship service each week. The fifth and sixth graders in one youth club worked with the director of music to put on musical plays such as "Fat Fat Jehosephat" and "We, Like Sheep."

There is an enrollment fee, and scholarships are available. Parents attend an annual orientation session and must serve in some aspect of the program at least three times each term. Some prepare the evening meal or clean up. Others help with crafts, music, or Bible study. Still others serve for a full term as hosts at one of the family-style dinner tables. They get to know the children at their tables and provide a familylike continuity to the fellowship there. In an age when many families are dysfunctional, this is a crucial aspect of the program.

Other adults from the congregation participate in leadership. The first director, for example, was not one of the parents. He was recruited because of his organizing and leadership ability as well as for his commitment to the program. A youth club must enlist scores of parents and other volunteers. That is the secret of its success. A positive, enthusiastic, and well-organized lay leader must be in charge. The director must not be afraid to ask people to serve. It helps to remind parents and church members of their vows during infant baptism. The pastor must be supportive and personally involved. Often this will be in teaching one of the Bible study classes or in eating regularly with the children.

To avoid burnout and to pass the leadership around, there is a new youth club director each year. Several assistants are preparing for this responsibility.

Trinity began the program by sending five or six carefully selected leaders to a training program. They came back all fired up. The program started on a snowy afternoon with fifty children and has grown to 150. Fellowship Church introduced the program with a sample afternoon to which they invited all parents. Then they asked parents and children to commit themselves to a short series in the spring. When fall rolled around, everyone was ready to go.

Logos or similar programs introduce many parents to the ministries of the church. At Trinity almost every class of new members includes those who have come to the church through the youth club. One afternoon each term, youth can bring one of their friends. Many friends want to come back. Through them their parents come.

The pastor of Trinity Church is a passionate advocate for Logos. "It can work in a church of any size where there are from three to twenty students," he says. It has been the beginning of renewal in three congregations he has known.

CHURCH SCHOOL FOR CHILDREN

Sunday schools are an important part of the family-oriented programs in bonding churches. Most of the seventeen hundred members in Grace Church are retirees. Nevertheless, the church has a strong commitment to its ministry with youth and children. They have an excellent educational program. The director of education recruits teachers individually on the basis of their potential. She persuades new members to help. Teachers commit themselves for one year at a time. New teachers receive training and work with an experienced teacher until their capabilities become clear.

The church carries on an active midweek program involving about eighty children and young people from second grade through high school. The music director and the director of education work together in a close partnership. The program includes choirs, bell choirs, and study. They use the Presbyterian and Reformed Education Ministry (PREM) denominational curriculum and other materials in a loosely graded program three afternoons a week: Grades 2–5 on Tuesday with about twenty-five children; grades 6–8 on Wednesday with close to thirty young people; and grades 9–12 on Thursday with about thirty.

Middle school and high school youth enjoy a supper prepared by volunteers, most of whom are senior citizens. They participate in denominational summer conferences and in work camps, described elsewhere. The program is successful in holding older students that drop out in many congregations. Out of twelve high school seniors, eight have participated consistently in the life of the church in spite of time conflicts with band, sports, and part-time employment. Chapter 10 will deal more completely with the importance of youth programs.

CHILDREN IN WORSHIP

The experience of congregational worship is an important part of a child's spiritual development. However, churches need to face squarely the problems parents have when their children participate in Sunday worship. Bonding churches help in several ways:

A SATURDAY WORKSHOP ON BAPTISM AND COMMUNION for parents and children prepares children for participation in the Lord's Supper. It helps parents feel comfortable about their doing so.

A CHILDREN'S VERSION OF THE SUNDAY WORSHIP BULLETIN with activities for the little ones is helpful.

"THE SMALL CHILD IN THE PEW" is a leaflet in the pew racks that helps older members understand and accept the presence of wiggly ones.

AN ACOLYTE CLASS for parents and selected children in the fourth through the sixth grades teaches responsibility to the church and to self. In four hour-long sessions they study worship and the communion service. They learn about liturgical colors at the pulpit and lectern, the changing of banners in the sanctuary, and the duties of an acolyte. Each Sunday a different child lights both candles and sits on the front pew. During the last hymn the acolyte relights the taper, puts out the candles, and carries the light of Christ out into the world. After the service acolytes pick up bulletins and straighten up the sanctuary. If they forget their good behavior, they are temporarily removed from the schedule.

MINISTRIES TO COUPLES AND TO PARENTS

The success of programs for children depends upon involvement of parents. Young couples and parents have important needs that bonding churches seek to meet. Some programs for parents are:

A YOUNG MOTHERS' BIBLE STUDY can become a strong support group and strengthen the spiritual lives of mothers. Many of their husbands do not participate in the life of the church.

A PARENTS' SUPPORT GROUP can be a valuable supplement to the youth club.

PROVISION OF CHILD CARE whenever needed makes an essential contribution to the participation of young parents in church programs.

MOTTO ("MOM'S TUESDAY TIME OUT") is a cooperative venture sponsored by the church. It allows mothers to leave their children with supervised care each Tuesday. Mothers give one Tuesday a month to care for all the children.

FINALLY, A DRUG AND ALCOHOL ABUSE PROGRAM is helpful to many parents who struggle with teenage at-risk behavior.

NEEDED: A REALISTIC UNDERSTANDING OF THE FAMILY

Parents need education in family life. The church is in an excellent position to provide it. Most young parents today grew up with many hours of television programs that have shaped their images of family. Many of those images are grossly unrealistic.

In his brilliant analysis of the baby-boom generation, Landon Jones points out that on television

> People did not work regularly but were rarely hungry or in need. . . . There was little unemployment . . . and no food stamps. Fathers were not wage earners but hapless buffoons, outwitted by both their children and their wives.
>
> . . . The television series . . . were relentlessly programming a vision of the American family that was either unrealistic or unattainable. No one . . . is ever alone. . . . There is little real despair. Problems can be worked out and almost always are. More TV parents are widowed than divorced. Anger is cute, rarely ugly. A child who would believe television would believe that most problems are soluble, usually within the half hour, and that sacrifices and compromises rarely involve human pain.[2]

Couples at Pleasant Lake Church eagerly respond to marriage retreats. In small groups they learn to apply the insights of their faith to marriage and family issues they are facing. As a large congregation, it can provide separate retreats for the particular needs of different age groups: twenty to thirty-five, thirty-five to fifty, and over fifty. Small churches can cover a broader age span or join with other churches in the community to meet the particular needs of people at different stages in family development.

Even a church of a hundred members can do something about parent education. The pastor of Plainfield Church saw the need for help to parents in his congregation and in the community. He went to a family life workshop and prepared himself to teach an Active Parenting class. The community education program agreed to cosponsor the class. Eight members of his congregation took the course along with ten others from the community.

The Sunday morning Active Parenting class at Trinity Church is usually overbooked. In addition to the standard materials for the course, they use supplementary material developed by Frieda Gardner of Princeton Seminary. This relates the insights of the Christian faith to different sections of the course.

RESOURCES FOR FAMILY NURTURE OF FAITH

The *Effective Christian Education* study showed that one of the most powerful influences in the development of faith maturity is discussion of faith by parents and their children. Bonding churches have encouraged this in several ways:

AT AN ORIENTATION FOR CHURCH SCHOOL PARENTS, the church encourages them to sign a covenant between themselves and God. In it they acknowledge that they are the primary teachers of the faith to their children. The church is just a partner in that calling.

FAMILY BIBLE STUDY is encouraged by giving Bibles to third graders in the middle of the year instead of at the end. This allows time to teach families how to use them. The Sunday following the presentation, parents and children come to a one-session class on how to use the Bible to nurture children in the home.

CHILDREN JOIN THEIR PARENTS' BIBLE STUDY GROUP every other Friday night. Parents and children participate together in modeling family devotions.

A BIBLE STUDY CURRICULUM for use in the home takes ten minutes a day. The director of children's ministry at Ocean View Church developed material that a hundred families used in the first quarter after it was introduced.

TAKE-HOME LEAFLETS FROM THE CELEBRATE CURRICULUM deal with the Bible passages that the children are studying in Sunday school. For grades three through six, there are devotional materials that parents can use for family prayers.

A LENTEN GUIDE ON SHALOM (PEACEMAKING) AND AN ADVENT BOOKLET developed by a Christian education director, provide resources for parents to use in family devotions. These have included activities that parents can do with children. The Celebrate and Shalom materials were helpful in developing those resources.

A BOOMING SINGLES MINISTRY

All people need the support of a family-type relationship, whatever their marital status. As he began his ministry at Ocean View Church, the pastor knew that the church must find a way to minister to the needs of singles. He felt the pain of widows and widowers who had lost a loving spouse. He saw the struggle of single parents seeking to be both father and mother to a growing family. He sensed feelings of bitterness and failure over broken marriages. He understood the longings of other singles for satisfying relationships.

He kept trying to start a singles program but was unable to find the right leader. One day she came along, and the program took off like a rocket. He now sees the singles ministry as one of their important strengths.

Every second and fourth Sunday evening between two hundred and three hundred singles come from all over the county. Most are between the ages of thirty-five and fifty. Perhaps one-fourth of them worship at Ocean View Church otherwise. There are fourteen hundred on the mailing list, and forty or fifty new people come to every meeting. There is a big turnover in attendance.

Two of the group, a man and a woman, coordinate the program. Jointly, a man and a woman lead each of five teams responsible for program, social events, communication, small groups, and outreach.

The Sunday night programs feature dynamic guest speakers on issues of particular concern to singles. Special events include retreats, seminars, and service projects. There are parties, dances, excursions, and sports. There are small groups for Bible study and socializing.

A DIVORCE RECOVERY WORKSHOP meets on six Monday evenings twice a year. It draws from fifty to eighty participants each series since 95 percent of those in the singles program are divorced. They know they need help. So this is an important part of the singles ministry. Two licensed marriage and family therapists lead the workshop. They cover such subjects as the stages of the divorce experience, coping with your ex-spouse, moving toward recovery, relating to yourself, and relating to others. The singles pastor leads a session on finding and experiencing forgiveness.

Each session begins with a one-hour presentation followed by discussion in small groups. Each small group is co-led by a man and a woman who have been through divorce. They are selected because they have been through healing, they are professing Christians, and they know how to facilitate a group.

The church also offers a program for the children of divorced parents.

A SINGLE-PARENTS' GROUP draws from fifteen to twenty-five people. A single parent leader works with a committee to plan their meetings. One meeting they have a speaker. The next they meet as a support group. A sponsoring couple provides stability to the discussion of parenting.

In all of these activities, the singles pastor seeks to maintain a low profile. She does lead the singing at the Sunday night program. Otherwise she is there to recruit, train, resource, and appreciate the team leaders. She meets with the coordinators every week or two and with the team leaders every month.

OTHER PATTERNS FOR SINGLES MINISTRIES

The size of the singles program at Ocean View Church is possible because the church is in a suburban community of a large metropolitan area. Many singles live there. In smaller population centers the needs of singles may be even more acute and resources less available. Fortunately, a singles program need not be large.

The pastor of Broadview Church recognized the unmet needs of the widows and widowers in that congregation. One of them was well on the way to working through her loss. Late in the fall he asked her to start a singles support group. "I'll do it after the holidays," she agreed.

"Do it now," he urged. "Holidays are the worst time. That's when people need it most." She started the group.

Nine or ten widows and two or three widowers now meet once a month for mental, psychological, and spiritual support. "When a spouse dies," one of them told us, "people have a tendency to go into a hole and to withdraw from life." So the group works hard to get those with a recent bereavement to join them. Members have helped each other in handling finances, taxes, nutrition, medical problems, and changes in former roles.

At one meeting a widow said, "I want to talk about assertiveness." She told of standing in line at a store. A man moved in front of her. "I believe I was next in line," she said. He looked at her. She broke into tears and left without getting what she came for.

Another told of how she and her husband used to meet socially with several other couples. After he died, she was no longer invited to join them. She asked one of them for an explanation. The reply startled her. "The table would not come out even," the woman said.

One congregation held a Saturday morning grief workshop with an outside resource person from a neighboring medical center. They listed the event in the community calendar and put up posters in the area. About forty-five people attended, half of them not members of the congregation. Out of that has grown a widows' support group.

There are many possibilities. If there are only a few singles, they could meet informally for lunch every other Sunday noon after church. Or they could meet twice a month on a weeknight. A joint singles program could be developed with a neighboring church or with a group of churches in the area.

Intergenerational events, described in other chapters, provide the potential for meeting some of the family fellowship needs of singles as they participate with children and adults of all ages and marital conditions.

HOW TO BEGIN

To begin a singles ministry, identify in your constituencies all singles of all ages and circumstances. Invite them to a special event, like a Sunday brunch or supper. Send written invitations and contact individuals by phone. Make clear that this is an occasion to discover how the church can serve singles more effectively. At the event, plan ways to discover what needs the church might meet for singles who respond and for those in the congregation or in the community who are not present. This may lead to one or more singles programs, depending on the needs that emerge.

This chapter closes with a positive philosophy for developing a singles ministry. It is in the form of an invitation from Mary Graves, associate pastor of the Solana Beach Presbyterian Church, to participate in their "Shipmates" program:

> Whether you are single by choice or not, your years of being a single adult are a great time of opportunity and growth. It doesn't have to be a time of waiting or loneliness, but can be a time of meaning and community. That is what we are about in Shipmates!
>
> It is our firm belief in Shipmates that you do not need to be married to have a family. And you do not need to be married to experience intimacy and companionship—or to be whole and fulfilled. These things are yours in the fullness of God's love offered to us in Jesus Christ.
>
> Shipmates is a PLACE for single adults to gather in a loving and non-judgmental atmosphere. It is a FAMILY of single adults building friendships and learning and laughing together. It is a FELLOWSHIP, a bonding together that is centered around God's goodness and grace. And Shipmates is an open door for single adults to know that they are welcome and included in Christ's CHURCH, the Family of God.
>
> Consider yourself invited to this active and loving gathering of single adults. This is one place where you don't need to feel bad about walking in the door alone. You are welcome here![3]

QUESTIONS FOR STUDY AND DISCUSSION

1. How many families with children living at home do you have in your congregation? How many of these are young families with small children? What proportion of your membership do families repre-

sent? What proportion of families like that are there in the community your church serves? What does this tell you about the importance of family-oriented ministries in your church?

2. What family-oriented programs does your church have? How effectively do those programs serve the needs of families in your church and in the community? What possibilities do you see in this chapter such as the crib connection, preschool, youth club, children in worship, ministries to parents, or family devotions?

3. What proportion of your congregation are single adults? Widows or widowers? Divorced? Single parents? Never marrieds? What proportion of the community served by your church is made up of singles? In what ways do you minister to singles? How might those ministries be improved?

RESOURCES

Celebrate. Presbyterian Publishing House, 100 Witherspoon Street, Louisville, KY 40202-1396. (800) 554-4694.

Gardner, Frieda. *A Biblical and Theological Guide to the Active Parenting Program*. Louisville, Ky: Office of Family Ministries, Presbyterian Church (U.S.A.), 1987.

Jones, Landon Y. *Great Expectations: America and the Baby Boom Generation*. New York: Coward, McCann & Geoghegan, 1980.

The Logos Program Associates. Youth Club Program, Inc. 1405 Frey Road, Pittsburgh, PA 15235. (412)372-1341.

Popkin, Michael H. *Active Parenting Handbook*. Atlanta: Active Parenting, Inc., 1983. Write to 810 Franklin Court, Suite B, Marietta, GA 30067.

Presbyterian and Reformed Education Ministry. Education and Congregational Nurture Ministry Unit, Presbyterian Church (U.S.A.), 100 Witherspoon Street, Louisville, KY 40202-1396. (800)334-6580.

10

EMPOWER YOUTH

It is a frightening cliché to say that young people are the future of the church. In congregation after congregation we watch our young people slip quietly out the back door. The average age of church members in mainline congregations increases each year. A sea of greying heads greets many a preacher each Sunday morning. If our offspring predict our future, what future does the church have?

The exodus of middle class youth and young adults between the ages of eighteen and thirty contributes most to membership loss in mainline denominations. Those are volatile years of struggle for self-identity and independence from parental restraints and inherited values.

Over the past twenty-five years the importance of church involvement among young Americans has been declining steadily but gradually. Each generation of young people in recent decades has entered adulthood with a lower level of church attendance than the previous generation. The *Effective Christian Education* study confirmed what most pastors already knew:

> Active involvement in Christian education is particularly weak at grades 10–12 and during adulthood. If nothing matters more than Christian education, then the weakest link in promoting faith and loyalty occurs here—a failure to draw adolescents and adults into the sphere of Christian education.[1]

It is not enough to sit back, accept the exodus, and reassure ourselves that youth will come back when they get married and have children. We may not be able to count on this. Indeed some of the baby-boom generation is beginning to return. But many young people do not come back at all. Many still affirm their faith in God and in Jesus Christ but have no use for organized religion. They find the church boring and irrelevant. They are disillusioned with the church and with all institutions.

Effective youth programs can make a difference. We found that key members of bonding churches are more likely than members in high-loss churches to name youth programs among the three most important contributors to membership retention. In fact it is the second most frequently mentioned program or approach. The United Presbyterian study titled *Membership Trends* found that growing congregations had more young people and programs for them than did declining churches.

Group Publishing, an organization that provides youth ministry resources, studied twenty rapidly growing churches. Their worship attendance averaged between 180 and five thousand.[2] Nearly three-quarters of members surveyed said that youth ministry was "very important" in their continuing involvement in the church. And 68 percent said they would reconsider their church membership if the youth ministry "fell apart or folded." We conclude that the retention of members in many churches requires a strong emphasis on pre-teen Christian education and effective programs for youth and young adults. Fortunately there are many successful youth programs in both large and small churches.

YOUNG CHRISTIANS IN SERVICE

Suburban First Church, outside a large eastern city, has five hundred members and a very effective youth program. Its high school students are deeply involved in the life of the church. Most graduates who remain in the community continue that involvement into young adulthood.

Their youth program is called "Christians In Service" (CIS). It depends on a close partnership between the young people and a group of caring adults. It derives much of its dynamism from an annual summer mission project, which both adults and young people eagerly await throughout the year. It maintains a balance between study, fellowship, and service. The young people themselves take the lead through five committees: Sunday school, fellowship, service, summer mission project, and fund-raising (to cover the costs of the summer trip).

A young person and an adult co-chair each committee and serve on a steering committee that coordinates the program. Early in the school year the young people select the mission project. Those who want to be involved are expected to participate actively in other aspects of the program. The steering committee makes the final decision on who will go. Young people themselves decide what adults to invite.

Sunday school is central to the program. About nine of the twelve senior high young people participate. The church considers this study so important that it does not ask its youth to teach other Sunday school classes.

During the year the youth group meets for planned fellowship every other Sunday evening. Informally, they gather on Wednesday and Friday evenings from seven o'clock to nine o'clock to play pool or ping pong or do homework together. Some bring friends, and some of those visitors later come to Sunday school and become active in the whole program. Some parents of those young people have come to church and become members of the congregation.

Service projects during the year have included leaf raking for the elderly, adopting a grandparent, working in the church nursery, ushering, and helping at the recycling center. They have shared in preparations for the congregation's birthday party for Jesus.

Two out of three years the summer mission project involves one week at a nearby location. One year teams of adults and young people together built a house for Habitat for Humanity. Another year they taught a vacation Bible school in a remote national missions community. Every third year the project lasts for two weeks and involves more expensive travel. The group selects its projects from those recommended by the national church and the presbytery.

Recently seven young people and five adults traveled by air from the East Coast to Colorado. They worked in a former mining community where there is a national park. First, they painted the home of an elderly widow and the picket fence of a neighbor. For nearly two weeks the group helped the National Forest Service convert a junkyard near a lake into a fishing area for the handicapped. They cleared sage brush and moved building materials to a new storage area. Adults and young people worked side by side. Together they shopped for food, prepared the meals, and did other daily chores. They lived together in the local youth center.

Each morning either a young person or an adult led devotions. About every third evening, there was a half-hour Bible study led by a couple of the adults. The group had "family meetings" to deal with individual or group concerns. One adult shared a burden from her personal life, and a young person prayed that she might find peace and let go of her problem. On Sunday they worshiped in the little church in the local community.

And, of course, they had lots of fun. There was bowling, horseback riding, a nature hike, white-water rafting, and a Fourth of July fireworks display. The local church hosted an ice cream social. They enjoyed a western opera, accompanied by all the boos and hisses that audiences love so much. There were visits to Pike's Peak, Aspen, and the Air Force Academy.

Each participant paid fifty dollars. Two from the same family paid seventy-five dollars for both. The balance of ten thousand dollars was raised during the preceding year by the young people, their parents, and adult leaders. They had an apple pie bake, pizza party, car wash, bake sale, and sold over a thousand handmade Chrismon ornaments. The fund-raising committee sold ten-dollar shares in the project. Contributors received a shareholder's certificate, and the young people sent them postcards. Finally, shareholders came to a special brunch and saw slides of what the group had done.

As one adult participant exclaims with confident enthusiasm, "None of the young people who participate in the CIS program will ever be the same again. Their lives are transformed!" No one could doubt that while looking into the radiant face of a high school senior. Because of her experience she vows to serve people for the rest of her life.

PRINCIPLES FOR EFFECTIVE YOUTH WORK

From this and other youth programs, we suggest the following principles for an effective ministry to youth.

Develop a Long-term Partnership Between Young People and Caring Adult Members

Eight of twelve seniors in Grace Church have participated consistently in church life. The director of Christian education ascribes their success to two things. First, there is a continuity of relationships with staff and with adult volunteers. For twelve years she has worked closely with the children as they have grown into young people. Her husband and another adult volunteer have given consistent help.

Richard Ross, youth coordinator of the Southern Baptist Sunday School Board, affirms the importance of this principle:

> Young people live with continual change in their lives. They are in love and out of love. Their friendships come and go. What holds a young person in the life of the church is the perception that people really care about them—that they have a relationship with someone with whom they feel secure and affirmed, who honestly wants them to grow.
>
> How does an adult build that kind of relationship? Intentionally! Watch for opportunities to be with them and to talk with them. At a youth picnic the adult sponsor has two options. You can stand talking with other adults at the refreshment table and watch the young people play volleyball. Or you can get in with the young people and play with them. Following a youth fellowship meeting, when you are tired and ready to go home, go the second mile. Say to some young person, "Come home with us." Go with young people to the youth conference.

Say by your actions, "I will do what is necessary to build a relationship with you."[3]

One congregation asks each participant in the confirmation class to choose an adult sponsor. Sponsors meet with their young partners regularly and keep informed as to what is happening in the class. Sponsors help them develop their statement of faith. This approach can be used in even the smallest congregation. It can forge a lasting partnership between a young person and a caring adult.

CULTIVATE CHRISTIAN COMMUNITY

Secondly, the Grace Church youth program is successful because it develops a noncompetitive, accepting community. That is different from all the rest of the lives young people lead at school, in sports, in band, and so on.

Genuine respect for young people and their concerns is of prime importance. "Our society doesn't take young people seriously," one youth minister points out. "Learn to listen to them. Many come from broken homes or dysfunctional families. They rarely find anyone who will really listen to what they have to say. Set aside your own agenda and be present for them with reflective listening."

Still another skilled youth worker says:

> Youth are on a roller-coaster ride every day with their feelings. Everything that happens is big to them. Their personalities are changing, and their hormones are playing dirty tricks on them. . . . Their number-one focus is on themselves, and the question they are asking is "Who am I?" Their constant concerns range from "How do I look?" to "Who cares?"
>
> They struggle with emotions—feelings of rejection, fear, and hurts that many times they do not share with anyone.[4]

Young people need affirmation, love, and self-esteem. They are often unsure of themselves and need to know that they are accepted as they are, not for what they achieve. One youth worker puts it to them this way, "God loves you, as *you*." Another pastor, whom I quoted in *Congregations Alive*, said, "What made Jesus so attractive to those who knew him was his willingness to see them for their possibilities rather than their past. What he did was to hold before them a vision of what they might become, rather than a picture of what they had been."[5]

This picture of grace as a way of life is especially applicable to young people. Operationally they can experience such acceptance in many ways. Ross suggests:

A positive climate of affirmation of young people—of believing in them—is essential. Too many adults in churches emphasize the negative when they talk about or talk to young people. They uplift the mistakes, the immorality, the drugs, and assume that young people are sexually irresponsible. Culturally, young people get loaded down with negatives. If they get another dose of negativity at church, they are likely to drop out.

Expression of interest after an absence is even more crucial with young people than with adults. When they have been absent, they will ask themselves, "Does anybody notice?" Teen-agers live so completely in the present that the only thing that matters is what happens *right now!*[6]

Adults who work with young people need to understand and to love them with genuine affection. They need to be willing to make a long-term commitment to working in partnership with them. A sense of humor about themselves is essential. Objectivity and firmness can keep them from becoming rescuers when confrontation is the most helpful course of action.

DEVELOP A BALANCED PROGRAM EMPHASIZING INVOLVEMENT IN SERVICE TO OTHERS

We found that effective youth programs in bonding churches have four major elements: study, service, fellowship, and involvement in the total life of the church.

STUDY. It is critically important to involve youth in the church school and other opportunities for study and questioning of their faith. The youth program of one denomination describes the first of five intentions of youth ministry this way:

We are called to discipleship by Jesus Christ. We respond to that call both individually and as members of a community. As individuals, we answer that call by accepting Jesus Christ as our Lord and Savior, publicly acknowledging our commitment to follow Christ, and then being obedient to God. Becoming a disciple means taking risks, meeting others' needs, and adopting a lifestyle that includes Bible study, prayer, worship, and service.

We need to give young people a place and time to question their faith, to explore what it means to follow Jesus in their own lives. This can be done through Bible study, worship and studying the lives of

Christians and other faithful people. . . . It means helping young people talk about their faith, within the church and with people outside the church.[7]

This is where the close continuing relationship with a caring adult really matters. Through reflective listening, a trusted adult can encourage young persons to express their doubts. As mentors they can share their faith and model a consistent, well-rounded Christian life. Thus, young people can discover a faith of their own. Authenticity of Christian faith and life in the adult model is key.

SERVICE. Young people are eager to give themselves to something that makes a difference in the world. They want to act out the gospel. Service projects provide an ideal opportunity for the church to channel the general disillusionment of young people into avenues for positive change. Through such involvement, intertwined with worship and deep sharing, they can more readily discover their own faith.

The *Effective Christian Education* study concludes, "Most adolescents in our churches are relatively uninvolved in service to other people, an experience which can serve not only as one antidote to at-risk behavior but can also be an important opportunity for spiritual growth."[8]

Youth programs can open doors for service. Guide a concern for hunger into taking part in CROP Walk or helping a food bank. Translate awareness of homelessness into framing a house through Habitat for Humanity. Get an equal number of retired adults to work with them. Bible study, issue discussion, and positive action can thus be channeled into faith development.

FUN AND FELLOWSHIP. Any successful youth program has times for play. Pool parties, beach parties, movies, camping trips, and other outings all have their place. They help build community. Young people get to know each other and their adult partners.

The junior high group at Broadview Church looks forward to Halloween with keen anticipation. They plan and set up a spook house for the children of the congregation. An imaginative woman who started the tradition works with them. They decorate the social hall with painted pumpkins and prepare refreshments. Parents bring their youngsters to the church where they play games and go trick-or-treating. Meanwhile, proud youth escort small groups of children through rooms that have been transformed into a haunted house.

Fellowship needs to be closely intertwined with everything that young people do. Many effective youth programs begin the school year with a retreat. This sets the tone for the year, deepens spiritual commitment, and builds relationships as new young people join the group. Trips, summer conferences, work projects are special opportunities for close companionship and recreation as well as for learning and growth in the faith.

Good Shepherd Church has a fall retreat in the mountains, a spring retreat at the shore, and a youth meeting every Sunday evening. Out of twenty-two church young people in grades seven to twelve, about sixteen participate in the Sunday evening program.

One Sunday evening a month is their ministry night. They may work in a soup kitchen, take dog food and supplies to an animal shelter, or prepare packages for prisoners. They paint their meeting room, straighten up the church, or clean the pews. One Sunday is a fun night.

They spend two Sundays in serious discussion and fellowship in someone's home. Parents fix a meal. Young people select their own topics or accept suggestions made by the director of Christian education, who meets with them. Subjects have included prayer, dating, drugs, teen-age sex, God, suicide, and capital punishment. A young person, an adult sponsor, or a visiting resource person is the leader.

INVOLVEMENT IN THE WHOLE CHURCH. Young people need to participate in the work of the whole church—locally, nationally, and internationally. Without preaching at them, this teaches the importance of a church community in their faith development. It can serve as an antidote to the strong trend among youth toward individualism and toward a divorce of faith from church activity. For example, studies have found that the strong institutional emphasis in Catholic religious instruction leads to a greater church involvement of Catholics in later years.

Locally, participation can come through singing in choirs, leadership in worship, and representation on boards and committees. Our study found that bonding churches are more likely than high-loss churches to involve young people in those ways. Intergenerational programs also effectively involve youth in the overall life of the church.

Most of the young people in Good Shepherd Church plan and conduct the annual youth Sunday. For several Sunday evenings and on one Sunday morning before that event, they work with the D.C.E. to plan the order of worship. They do the children's sermon, and three of them give "Thoughts" in place of a sermon. Some prepare the special music. Others usher and take up the offering. That Sunday in May is when the congregation honors its graduating seniors.

One of the highlights of the year in many youth programs is to join young people from other churches in district retreats, regional summer conferences, the Montreat International Youth Summer Conference, or the national Triennial Youth Meeting. They meet young people from all over the country and from around the world. Their horizons are lifted and the glorious diversity of the church of Jesus Christ becomes the warm flesh and blood of other vibrant young people.

INVOLVE PARENTS

The *Effective Christian Education* study found that "the two most powerful connections to faith maturity for youth are family religiousness and lifetime exposure to formal Christian education." As these increase, so does faith maturity. Other less powerful factors that promote faith maturity among youth are "lifetime church involvement, the religiousness of best friends, the lifetime experience of a caring church, lifetime involvement in serving others, and non-church religious activities."[9]

> The particular family experiences most tied to greater faith maturity are the frequency with which an adolescent talked with mother and father about faith, the frequency of family devotions, and the frequency with which parents and children together were involved in efforts, formal or informal, to help other people. Each of these family experiences is more powerful than the frequency with which an adolescent sees his or her parents engage in religious behavior like church attendance.[10]

On the other hand, Richard Ross believes that family participation in the life of the congregation can be more important than anything else in holding young people in the church. Over time children tend to take on the pattern of their parents. Parental attendance and commitment provide a model for their children. Young people who are alone in their involvement in the church are likely to drop out, he tells us. We may need to say to parents, "If it is part of your dream for your young person to be nurtured in the Christian faith, you need to lead the way."[11]

HELP YOUNG PEOPLE COPE WITH AT-RISK BEHAVIOR

Two frightening findings emerged from the *Effective Christian Education* study. First, a majority of youth in mainline churches engage in at-risk behavior. Second, churches are doing much too little to deal with this reality. The study developed a ten-point at-risk index. It defined at-risk behavior as engaging in one of the following behaviors during the previous twelve months:

Depression twenty or more times

Thought about suicide once or more

Alcohol use six or more times

Binge drinking: got drunk three or more times

Marijuana use three or more times

Cocaine use once or more

Aggression: hit or beat up someone six or more times

Theft: shoplifted three or more times

School trouble three or more times

Sexual intercourse once or more (whether or not in the previous twelve
    months)[12]

They found that "the percentage of all mainline youth with at least one
at-risk indicator increases from 66 percent of 7th and 8th graders to 80% of
11th and 12th graders."[13] Percentages of young people in the eleventh and
twelfth grades with three or more at-risk indicators ranged in different mainline denominations from 27 percent to 54 percent. They found that 42
percent of boys and 46 percent of girls had been intoxicated at least once in
the past twelve months. Sadness and depression are frequent experiences.

The study concludes that "Many congregations do not address these adolescent realities in particularly powerful or significant ways. Only a minority,
for example, place high emphasis on service to others, sexuality education, or
chemical education. By missing these opportunities to connect faith to life,
congregations may thwart the development of faith and loyalty."[14] Indirectly,
the young people themselves say this. Less than half of them said that they
had "learned something important" at their church.

How then can our youth programs help people deal with at-risk behaviors?
Ross suggests:

The twelve-step recovery programs developed by A.A. but used in so
many other ways are useful. They manifest a clear perception of how
we are put together and are consistent with scripture. A great deal can
be learned by incorporating those principles in working with teenagers. Young people who are into drugs are not happy. They are miserable. Those who are sexually irresponsible are not happy. They are
miserable.[15]

In order to provide parents and young persons with resources to deal with at-risk behavior, Broadman Press has developed *The 24-Hour Counselor*. This is a series of forty-eight crisis tapes. For each of twelve subjects there are four albums (three for youth and one for parents). Christian psychologists have prepared the tapes to help deal with teenagers' crises. Those who buy them have permission to make unlimited copies. Without embarrassment, a young person or a parent can pick up a tape from a wall display or the church library. Others need not know the problems they are facing. Ross estimates that as many as half a million teenagers are using the tapes.[16]

HOLD CONFIRMATION CLASSES FOR SEVENTH AND EIGHTH GRADERS

The timing and character of confirmation classes is important. The United Presbyterian *Membership Trends* study discovered that, in contrast with declining churches, growing churches were more apt to have a regularly scheduled confirmation class. They confirmed young people at an earlier age.

We found that bonding churches are more likely than high-loss churches to have regularly scheduled confirmation/membership classes. Very small churches may need to hold such classes every other year or when their children reach a suitable age.

Something can be said for waiting to enroll young people in a confirmation class until they are ready for it. However, our study suggests that young people should participate in a confirmation class no later than the eighth grade. Bonding churches with more than two hundred members are more likely than high-loss churches of that size to have membership classes for young people in grades seven, eight, or lower. High-loss churches of that size are more likely to hold classes for grades nine or ten. Most churches with less than two hundred members favored the earlier age for confirmation classes.

We suggest that confirmation before the ninth grade may cultivate an informed faith commitment to the church before the times of greatest turmoil in adolescent development. That in turn may lead to a stronger bonding to the church.

RECOGNIZE POSSIBILITIES IN SMALL CHURCHES

Bonding churches in our study were more likely to have youth groups than high-loss churches. In small churches this difference was particularly notable. In churches with less than two hundred members, 68 percent of bonding churches had youth groups. Only 37 percent of small high-loss churches had such groups. This may be because many small high-loss churches do not have young people in their constituencies. However, it seems more likely that many small high-loss churches simply do not know how to meet the needs of the few young people they do have. They may just assume there is little they can do to minister to them. In fact, small churches have more than one option.

Some have enough young people to develop their own youth groups and to attract other neighboring young people. The 150-member Crossroads Church is known throughout the area for its strong youth program. In addition to a "junior youth program" for children from third through sixth grades, it attracts older young people. Twenty-seven youth from seventh through twelfth grades meet once a month in one of their homes for a meal, music, Bible study, and lots of fun. They support a child through an international children's program. Once a month their choir sings in the worship service. Part of the program's success is diligent support from lay leaders and dedicated parents who expect their young people to participate actively in church school and in the various youth activities.

Small churches with only a few young people can cooperate with other nearby churches in a joint program. A rural church with sixty-six members suddenly found itself near a new housing development, within commuting distance of a large metropolitan area. With judicatory help, the congregation began supporting a full-time pastor and a youth worker. Other denominations had not yet established churches there. So the church decided to start a community youth ministry that would serve young people regardless of their denomination.

Three years later the church has grown to 160 members. In partnership with other churches it continues to sponsor its youth groups. Up to thirty high school students meet weekly on Saturday or Sunday for recreation or study of some ethical, biblical, or theological subject of interest to the group.

Sixth to eighth graders meet each week for similar activities. The new Methodist church has withdrawn from this program because it now has a large enough junior high school group to start its own program. However, the Episcopal and Presbyterian churches have determined to continue joint programming for their young people.

Of course, this congregation has had the double advantage of a growing situation and outside financial resources. However, it does illustrate the way in which neighboring small churches can develop joint youth programs. The relational model of youth ministry holds great potential for small churches. As Lea Appleton notes, a committed adult in a very small congregation can engage in youth ministry with small groups of from two to ten: "This size has possibilities for intimate discussion, personal sharing, and one-on-one interaction between young people and adults. You can get to know young people well and share their joys and fears. Become their friend, and they will become yours."[17]

A church can minister meaningfully to even one lone young person. It takes one dedicated adult willing to be a friend and mentor. Once a month get together for breakfast and Bible study. Take the young person to a district youth rally. Make it possible for the young partner to attend a summer conference or work camp. Use your imagination to discover other opportunities for that person's development. All these can be youth ministry in a very small church.

Some small churches with a few older young people involve them in leadership of programs for younger children such as their youth clubs or in teaching a church school class. Such participation helps bond high school youth to the church, assists in their faith development, and provides role models for younger children.

Bridge the Transitions from Childhood Through Adolescence to Young Adulthood

Congregations need to give particular attention to two transition points in the development of their young members. The first is the transition from childhood to adolescence, which takes place during grades seven through twelve. Loss of young people begins then. That is the transition we have been dealing with here. Graduation from high school introduces a period of transition from adolescence to young adulthood. That most critical period for membership retention is the subject of the next chapter.

QUESTIONS FOR STUDY AND DISCUSSION

1. What young people of junior high and high school age do you have among the members of your congregation or their families? In the constituencies that your congregation serves? In the community you serve?

2. What youth programs do you have that serve these young people? How effective do you judge them to be? What proportion of these young people of different ages are participating in these programs? What does that suggest regarding changes you might consider? To what extent is your congregation meeting the needs of these young people?

3. If you do not have youth programs, what does this chapter suggest for future action?

4. Which of the principles for youth work in this chapter are already guiding your ministry to youth? Which might you begin to use? How might you implement those principles?

5. If you are part of a very small congregation and have only a very few young people, how might you minister to them? Who among your membership might be effective in carrying on that ministry? How can you challenge them to undertake it?

RESOURCES

Benson, Peter L., and Carolyn H. Eklin. *Effective Christian Education: A National Study of Protestant Congregations.* Minneapolis: Search Institute, 1990.

Ross, Richard, ed. *The Work of the Minister of Youth.* Nashville: Convention Press, 1989.

Strommen, Merton P. *Five Cries of Youth.* San Francisco: Harper & Row, 1988.

Talbot, Mary Lee, ed. *Guidebook for Youth Ministry in Presbyterian and Reformed Churches.* Philadelphia: The Geneva Press, 1988.

The 24-Hour Counselor. Tapes for dealing with at-risk behavior of youth. Nashville: Broadman Press. (800)458-2772.

11

SPAN THE YOUNG ADULT YEARS

The decline in the proportion of mainline Protestants in the population is due mainly to losses among young adults. A lower proportion of members of mainline Protestant denominations were under 30 in 1987 than in 1983, reflecting a continuation of a decades-long trend.

GEORGE GALLUP, JR., AND JIM CASTELLI, *THE PEOPLE'S RELIGION*[1]

The loss of young adults under thirty years of age is a critical problem for mainline denominations. This is part of a general trend in that segment of the population. Gallup polls find that they are "less interested and involved in religion than those over 30. For example, 58 percent of those over 30 and only 41 percent of those under 30 say that religion is 'very important' in their lives."

Most dropouts occur when members move. Young adults are among the most mobile segments of the population. Many young people lose interest in the church beginning in their middle teens. The one move that finally closes the door takes place when they graduate from high school. They leave home for college or work and leave the church behind. Those least likely to attend church are between the ages of eighteen and twenty-five. According to Roy Oswald and Speed Leas, they "are most likely to be critical of religious institutions and have negative images of organized religion."[2] In their late twenties or early thirties, when they do return to the church, they are apt to bring with them different values than those who have stayed in the church.

This has been true for baby boomers, born between 1945 and 1965. Many of them are still younger than thirty-five. In the '60s and '70s value changes took place in the direction of individualism, tolerance for diversity, and personal freedom. This made a telling impact on many boomers. Church commitment declined, and dropouts increased, particularly among middle-class young people and college-educated young adults. These are the normal constituencies of mainline churches.

Thirty-four percent of the boomers dropped out of church altogether, and

141

they have never returned. Twenty-one percent dropped out and later returned. Forty-one percent have remained in a church of some kind.[3]

We have already noted that young adults with children are coming back to churches that meet the needs of their families. We have seen how bonding churches minister to the widowed and divorced. We have also seen how they try to maintain contact with their mobile young adult members. All of this is important, but it is not enough.

Bonding churches are more likely than high-loss churches to have programs for young adults and singles. However, most of the young-adult programs are for couples with children, and most singles programs serve older adults. We found no bonding churches with a model for ministry to young singles. Where they attracted young singles, it was mainly to their worship services or to some intergenerational activities.

Accordingly, we sought and found several other churches that are successfully ministering to young singles. And we found a campus-ministry program that spans the faith commitment gap from home church to college.

BRIDGING THE FAITH CHASM

There was a day when campus ministries focused their energies on ministering to students. Then came a period when energies shifted to faculty and administration. The goal was to impact the structures of academia. Unfortunately, this shift came when large numbers of baby boomers were arriving on those campuses. When these young adults most needed to cross the faith chasm from the church back home to the freedom of the campus, the bridges were not there. This compounded the natural loss of young people during the post–high school period.

College is the time when young adults are challenging all life's assumptions, especially those of their own heritage. They seek to be their own person rather than a clone of someone else. They are intent on doing their own thinking and feeling. For some, it is a time of broad questioning. This is an important part of maturation. The church needs to be with them and encourage them in their quest. For others there is an eagerness to find authoritative answers.[4] The church needs to help them find those answers.

Fortunately we found a model that is highly suggestive of a direction the church might move to meet this challenge. The campus ministers on nine major campuses of a southern state have orchestrated a program that spans the faith pilgrimage of the early young adult years. It helps high school graduates make the transition from their home church to involvement in a campus ministry program and in a campus-related church.

Each year they conduct a statewide retreat for Presbyterian students in grades ten through twelve. Young people get to know the campus ministers who will be working with them when they go on to college. A Presbyterian college hosts the retreat. Young people get to know that campus and can consider studying there. College students from the different campuses lead the small group discussions. They get to practice their leadership skills, reinforce their own faith, and make friends with potential new college students.

The campus ministers get to know high school students by being active in their presbytery's youth councils. Their network shares information on what students are coming to which campus. Campus ministers contact each transfering student. Then, as they first arrive on campus, the local church holds a luncheon for them. Families from the congregation that have agreed to sponsor one of the students for the year are present. Students and families match themselves and begin a relationship that develops throughout the year.

A student center on one of those campuses illustrates what happens after that. Supported by the local presbytery, it provides facilities for recreation and other student activities. The program aims to involve students in the nearby church where the campus minister also serves as associate pastor. Students are highly visible in the congregation, often serving as liturgists in the services.

The campus ministry program has four foci:

A QUESTIONING MINISTRY. It challenges students to think through their faith. At a Sunday night supper, forty to fifty of them grapple with some issue they have previously chosen. They might have a visiting speaker or a student presentation. In a panel discussion, for example, a homosexual, an African American, and a disabled person describe their experiences with prejudice. After presentation of biblical material related to prejudice, they break into small discussion groups.

BIBLE STUDY. Two groups of eight students engage in study of the Kerygma Bible program. The campus pastor leads another group in a men's dormitory and a fourth group meets in a women's dormitory.

SERVICE-ORIENTED ACTIVITIES. A Habitat Club works each week on a home building project. Students participate in CROP Walk and help in a soup kitchen. They tutor English to Spanish-speaking children and work with underprivileged children in a recreational program.

"Young people today are idealistic," affirms the campus pastor.

They believe they can make a difference in the world. They will respond if you give them an opportunity to put their faith into action. In the process they discover how they feel about their faith and why. Service speaks to the heart and gives young people perspective to clarify what is really important. Their previous experiences have affirmed so many different values they need an opportunity through service to discover what counts.

FELLOWSHIP, FUN AND COMMUNITY-BUILDING ACTIVITIES. Students build lasting friendships as they enjoy a wide variety of recreational activities.

All this cries out for national and regional church bodies to assign major resources to campus programs. It challenges the church to develop ministries to students in their journey from childhood assent to adult faith maturity. Caring congregations need to learn how to provide continual support to their absent young adults in their questioning and life exploration. Some pastors make annual visits to students away at college. Some congregations keep absent young adults on an affiliate roll as a means of keeping in touch with them.[5] Whatever else is done, the church must build more bridges across the chasm between congregation and campus or distant place of work.

BOOMING YOUNG SINGLES PROGRAMS

We learned about four churches with successful young singles programs. Not surprisingly, all four were large churches in cities with significant numbers of young singles. They were in different parts of the country. By telephone we interviewed staff members in all four of them. We then visited one and interviewed a group of leaders in its singles programs.

A congregation of about nine thousand members in a large southern city has a dynamic young adult program. Ten years ago its Sunday school class for singles had been attracting more and more of the older singles—widows, widowers, and the divorced. Then about ten or fifteen of the younger singles decided to start their own group. "Let's do our own thing," they said. Twelve people were in the first class. Ten years later there is a regular Sunday morning attendance of between two hundred and 250 single adults between the ages of twenty and thirty-five. Three hundred from that class attended a covered-dish celebration of its tenth anniversary.

As we have said, ours is an era when many young adults are no longer involved in the church. What then draws so many of them to a church school class? Perhaps the name of their group gives a clue. They call themselves the "Roaring Twenties." The secret, says the associate pastor, is that the church has given them permission to do many radical things not normally associated with a church program. They get together somewhere on Friday evenings for a happy hour and hold monthly parties. They hold dances four or five times a year: a Christmas dance, a Mardi Gras dance, and a senior prom, for example. Twenty of the group now live together in an apartment complex, and there are several fellowship clusters within the larger group. "For Singles Only" is a weekly gathering with dinner and a program on such varied subjects as crime prevention or AIDS.

Each fall and spring the Roaring Twenties group sponsors retreats at two different resort areas. One of the pastors of the church goes on each retreat. Its spiritual content consists of a Sunday morning worship service on the beach. The rest of the time is for fun and relaxation. On a recent weekend 250 from one singles group went to one resort area and three hundred from four other singles groups went to another.

When it comes to reaching and holding young adults, that church must be doing something right. Two-thirds of its new members are single. Of those, more than one-third are young adults.

PRINCIPLES FOR WORKING WITH YOUNG SINGLE ADULTS

What are young adults seeking when they move tentatively toward the church? What are their perceived needs? What are their deeper unarticulated needs? Answers to these questions may help other churches minister more effectively to them.

Our answers come from three principal sources: first, from listening to young adults themselves and to those who work closely with them; second, from the work of Daniel Yankelovich as elaborated by Tex Sample in *U.S. Lifestyles and Mainline Churches;*[6] and third, from Robert Gribbon's book *Developing Faith in Young Adults.*

It is striking to discover how closely the main themes of the bonding churches coincide with the needs of young adults. They too seek fellowship, meaning for living, and opportunities for constructive service. Their search for intimacy expresses a need to belong. Yet they are not ready for long-term commitments.

Church leaders who seek to understand the complexity of the baby-boom generation will find Sample's analysis instructive. He interprets the differences between persons who are on the cultural left, cultural right, and cultural middle. It is not possible here to describe those three groups. Instead we have selected some characteristics in his description that fit information we gathered from the four churches.

Young Adults Long for Satisfying Relationships

"Young adults are hungry for fellowship and community with their peers," one of the pastors told us. "We open the door for them to find that fellowship under the sponsorship of the church. We give them permission to be themselves and to come to a recognition of their need."

The search for relationships can prove to be the point of entry to deeper spiritual lives. One young man confessed that he had started coming to the Roaring Twenties for purely social reasons. He wanted to meet young women. "As I participated in the program," he said, "things happened to me spiritually."

A young woman told of her pilgrimage: "I dropped out of church in the seventh grade when my parents stopped forcing me to go. When I got out of college, I felt the need for fellowship, so I came back. Now, at age thirty-three, I feel I have the spiritual maturity to make a lifelong commitment."

Successful programs build deep and lasting relationships. Young adults told us that the best bonding takes place outside the formal larger group in small informal settings such as meetings for lunch. "Intimacy," they said, "really comes in working together in service projects and in small week-night Bible study groups."

Young Adults Seek Self-Fulfillment

Daniel Yankelovich has found that as many as 80 percent of adults in the United States are in one way or another engaged in a search for self-fulfillment.[7]

By the seventies . . . Americans from every walk of life were suddenly eager to give more meaning to their lives, to find fuller self-expression and to add a touch of adventure and grace to their lives and those of others. Where strict norms had prevailed in the fifties and sixties, now all was pluralism and freedom of choice: to marry or live together; to have children early or postpone them, perhaps forever; to come out of the closet or stay in; to keep the old job or return to school; to make commitments or hang loose; to change careers, spouses, houses, states of residence, states of mind. . . .

The life experiments of self-fulfillment seekers often collide violently with traditional rules, creating a national battle of moral norms. Millions of Americans are hungry to live their lives to the brim, determined to consume every dish on the smorgasbord of human experience. But their appetites have scandalized other millions. . . .[8]

In its extreme forms the self-fulfillment ethic involves a preoccupation with self, a me-first approach to life, and a rejection of the self-denial ethic of previous generations. Yankelovich tells us that 17 percent of U.S. citizens live by this "strong-form" of self-expression.[9] They have seen the deprivation their parents suffered in denying themselves for the sake of their families or for others, and they will have none of it.[10]

Tex Sample, in his *U.S. Lifestyles and Mainline Churches,* points out that "the baby boomers have been the generation most characterized by the ethic of self-fulfillment." That also is the generation largely missing from the church. Those least likely to be part of the church are adherents of the strong form of self-expression. Sample calls them the core of the cultural left. He concludes that "the more strongly one holds to an ethic of self-fulfillment, the less likely one is to belong to the church."[11] Those most likely to be part of the church are the 20 percent residing in the United States who have not been affected by the self-fulfillment ethic. These Sample calls the cultural right.

Yankelovich estimates that 63 percent of people in the United States fall between the two extremes. The commitment of this majority to self-fulfillment is weak. They "retain many traditional values, including a moderate commitment to the old self-denial rules, even as they struggle to achieve some measure of greater freedom, choice and flexibility in their lives."[12] They have many other concerns in their lives than the search for self-fulfillment. These include "family obligations, work, inflation worries, health cares, kids with school problems, crime . . . " and so on.[13] Many baby boomers are in this group.

Our challenge, particularly when seeking to reach the baby-boom generation, is to discover how we can minister meaningfully to those in this latter group. This will not be easy, since many in the church have been most strongly influenced by the self-denial ethic.[14] Once, when explaining the differences between the self-denial ethic and the self-fullfillment ethic, Sample was interrupted by someone who said, "We will welcome these people when they become Christians. The scripture says that to do this 'one must deny himself, take up the cross, and follow Christ.'" Quickly a baby boomer replied, "It also says that Christ came that we might have life and have it more abundantly."[15]

How, then, do we reach the baby-boom generation? Among other things, by recognizing their concerns for self-fulfillment. Our interviews with some of them gave us clues: "Young adults expect quality in their programs, or they won't come," they told us. "If it isn't fun, don't do it. The Christian life is a deep running joy. God parties and celebrates with people."

A sense of self-fulfillment can come to young adults when they experience "psychological success." We described this in chapter 6. One pastor describes for us a style that helps people achieve it:

People support what they help create. Singles must run their own programs. Our task is to help them fulfill their dreams. Therefore we accept and trust them. We support and encourage them and assume they have much to contribute. Give them authority and expect responsibility.

Young Adults Are Wary of Long-term Commitment

Young adults need space to explore life and its options. They are hesitant to make long-term commitments until they are very sure of themselves. They are shoppers more than joiners. They shop for a career, for a life-style, for a spouse, or for a church. One experienced pastor who works with young adults recognizes that they do not easily commit themselves to a particular church. He says to them, "That's fine! What can we be for you? How can we enable you to be part of the body?"

Offer programs that require short-term commitments. We found Sunday school classes that regularly draw large numbers of young adults. Young adults themselves select the subjects they will study. They decide on the leaders who will resource them. Each subject is treated in a short series of class sessions. Because each subsequent subject has been chosen by the participants, another short-term commitment is possible. Thus a series of short-term program commitments results in a longer-term commitment to the class.

This in turn can lead to other commitments of longer duration. Several years ago some members of the Roaring Twenties group felt the need for a deeper spirituality. They started a Tuesday night gathering in which from thirty to a hundred are now engaging in a spiritual quest under the guidance of their resource persons. These include the pastors of the church and a doctor who is also a seminary graduate.

Sample puts the issue of commitment in helpful theological perspective:

> According to the gospel, God does not first require commitment. Instead, God acts in our behalf, sends Christ to live and die for us, and raises Christ as our promise and hope. Christian faith does not begin by telling us what we must do, but by proclaiming what God has already done. God first establishes a relationship through God's action. Only later when we trust and receive God's gift of grace in faith do we understand that true faith is active in love and justice and in acts of mercy and self-giving. At the very heart of the gospel is the dynamic in which relationship precedes commitment.[16]

Because of young adults' hesitancy to make commitments, a young-adult program needs to provide a balance between anonymity and intimacy. Some are eager for involvement. They want to be asked to do things. Others want to test the waters, try it out, see if they want to come in. They need a place to hide. So they prefer a large group. They do not want to walk in and get appointed to a job. This is one of the problems with a small young singles group. There are not enough people to make the group go without pouncing on new people and driving them away.

THE BIBLE, THE GOSPEL, AND WORSHIP ARE IMPORTANT TO YOUNG ADULTS

All those we interviewed were clear on one point. Young adults come to the church for more than social relationships. Strong biblically based programs are important. The gospel matters to them. Solid Bible teaching empowers them. They want to be like Christ and reach out to others. The Bible helps them do this. Programs should articulate what is essential in the Christian faith and relate it to issues young adults feel are important.

Let the Bible speak to the storms that people are facing. For example, after looking at the story of the woman taken in adultery, one class divided into small discussion groups. They asked, "How does this speak to us about friends who are caught in bad spots?"

Gribbon says, "We found young adults attracted by what they perceived as a living faith, convincingly believed and lived in relation to their world. We found that young adults who sought out the church were looking for a connection between transcendent reality and their day-to-day lives."[17]

Remember that people are at different spiritual levels. Many have not grown up in the church. They feel a lot of intimidation and hesitation when they come to a church group. People are looking for structure and for spiritual growth. Accept their differences without watering down the message. Help them discover meaning in the midst of the day-to-day realities they face.

A church . . . that welcomes strangers and other aliens as co-travelers on the way, and that faithfully and humbly claims Christ as Savior and Lord can be an authentic place to go to worship, learn, pray, and study, and from which to scatter to live, seek justice, make peace, and dream toward the transformation that God is bringing.[18]

Many congregations offer an alternative expression of worship on Sunday morning or at some other time in the week. This may meet some worship needs of those young adults who are unmoved by formal services. Sample suggests that services need to be emotionally expressive. They should "take greater advantage of silence, speak to the mystical, the therapeutic, the socially visioned dimension of people's lives—indeed, aim at a transformative event where God's grace is experienced in community and God's reign calls cultural-left boomers to new commitments."[19]

One church built an annual retreat for young adults around the theme of prayer and the spiritual life.

THEY SEEK LIFE DIRECTION AND CLARIFIED IDENTITY

One of the differences between youth and young adults is a shift toward a career orientation. Concerns emerge about occupational choices, success and failure, leadership, and the meaning of work in life. In larger metropolitan areas, especially with the upwardly mobile, there are anxieties over the best occupational choice among many choices that are available. In smaller communities concerns may center on limited occupational choices and a lack of opportunities for advancement.

Another difference, especially among young women, is a growing preoccupation with identity and role expectations of men and women. For women the biological clock begins to tick and the struggle between career and marriage occupies more and more attention. Who am I? Where am I going? What does it all add up to? These become important questions.

One congregation, located in an upwardly mobile residential community near the financial and commercial center of a large Midwestern city, has developed programs to deal with some of these concerns. A series of seven o'clock breakfast meetings at a downtown club draws from fifty to 120 young adults to discuss a variety of topics. Program titles have included "Am I Having Fun Yet?" (relationships and satisfaction in the work place and related spiritual concerns), "Ethics in the Work Place," and "Faith and Its Implications for Life and Work" (with a personnel manager, a judge, and a doctor as resources).

The church advertises each series widely. Young adults respond to advertising. Church groups distribute a brochure announcing each series. It is sent to two hundred young adults. The series is an opportunity for office evangelism as members who work downtown invite their friends.

Young Adults Want to Make a Difference in the World Through Service

Young adults take social issues seriously. They want to make a difference in the world. Expect them to give as well as receive. Many want very much to give their time, their abilities, and their money. Most want to be asked to do things. Invite them to help. Challenge them in concrete ways. Be very specific and give them opportunities for hands-on service. They will respond.

In one large city church, young adults cook for homeless shelters, build Habitat for Humanity homes, and rehabilitate public housing units. They tutor three hundred children and participate in work camps for young adults in Mexico and Arizona. Another church integrates service activities in everything they do. Service becomes a point of entry to the board of deacons and other offices in the church.

PROGRAMMING FOR YOUNG SINGLES

Begin by finding out how extensive your young adult constituency is. A large program is possible only if there are many young singles in the area you serve. This may then require major resources of a very large congregation or of several churches working together.

Invite the young adults in your church into your home. Ask them what approach would get them and their friends more involved in the life of the church? What are their needs? Design programs that speak to their needs and fit into their hectic schedules. They are going ninety miles an hour. Meal-related events and small group activities help in this. Build in as many options as possible.

Get the blessing of the congregation's governing body. Help them recognize how society has changed since they were younger. Remind them how Jesus ministered to those who did not conform to religious traditions. Convince them that the church needs to welcome young adults on their own terms.

Do not be afraid to try things and fail. Keep enough variety in your programs so that if one approach fails, others will keep up the momentum. Let young adults take the lead and get them to delegate responsibility to others. If two or three people do everything, the program will die.

Where a Large Group Seems Feasible

Young adults told us there is a magic number of about thirty people to make a large singles program go. This is a minimum to sustain itself when some do not show up. More than that introduces additional dynamics. Out of the thirty, there needs to be a core group of fifteen who participate every week. Fifteen others should be coming every other week or so.

Large churches in metropolitan areas may be able to develop young adult singles programs of their own. Other churches may have neither the location nor the resources to do this. If there are enough single young adults within their communities, a group of smaller churches might be able to attract a large enough group to mount such a program. Participants would continue to worship and serve in their own congregations.

A regional body of a single denomination, such as a presbytery or a conference, can group churches together and organize opportunities for young singles: social activities, summer conferences, retreats, and service projects.

It takes a lot of hard work by a few committed people to get a group started: calling visitors to get them to come back, getting interesting teachers, planning fun things.

The Roaring Twenties class started with twenty people the minister invited to his house for dinner. Out of that twenty, three stayed with the class. Two-and-a-half years later, there were about twenty coming to the class regularly. The class really took off when they started a Tuesday evening fellowship time "For Singles Only." This attracted many new members, and the class grew rapidly.

Reaching out to visitors and new members of the group is critically important. Greet them warmly when they come. Select greeters who have the gift to make people feel at home in the class. Make small talk. Remember their names. Follow up with telephone calls to get them to come back. Develop in the class an "outreach attitude."

Large programs must maintain intimacy through small groups. A class of forty found they were losing intimacy. For some activities they created subgroups composed of people from four categories: officers and other leaders, people who had been in the class a long time, people who had been in the class for two or three months, and those who were brand new to the class.

Where Large Young Singles Groups Are Not Possible

Most churches do not have enough young singles to form a large group. But in many there are at least a few young singles. Bring them together. Ask them what will meet their needs. A Bible class or other study program, managed by its participants, would probably prove to be important.

Involve young singles in the total life of the congregation. When they are ready, enlist them in places of responsibility. One of these might be in working with one of the younger youth groups or teaching in the Sunday school.

A survey of singles in one large program concluded, "Singles want to maintain their identity as not married and yet be included in the whole of the church family through interaction with those in older and younger age groups than themselves as well as married members and families."[20]

Some young adults live in relatively stable communities and have not gone to college. They may feel very much out of place in the church. One congregation of two hundred members in such a community encourages them to continue in the high school youth group and asks them to provide leadership for the younger teens. They have their own Sunday school class and assist as liturgists in worship services. This has encouraged some to continue to be actively involved in the life of the congregation.

Gribbon emphasizes working for the faith development of young adults rather than for the development of a young-adult program, as such. He suggests four things that any congregation can do to minister to them: Be there for them even when they do not feel the need to participate; affirm both the questions and the questioners; provide mentors and peers (they need "to be significantly engaged with believing and believable adults"); and believe vibrantly and authentically. Offer hope for the future.[21]

In Conclusion

Tex Sample wrote the following words for those on the cultural left. However, they give us a thoughtful summary of what the church needs to do if it is to carry on a viable ministry to most single young adults:

> Church programming, then, with the cultural left begins by looking for niches in their lives where the church can offer a ministry that provides an intrinsically valuable experience of worship, one that is emotionally expressive, that opens up the opportunity for new relationships, and that can deliver out of this, occasions for short-term, hands-on servant ministry to the world.[22]

QUESTIONS FOR STUDY AND DISCUSSION

1. How many college students or other absent young adults are on the membership rolls of your church? What is your church doing to maintain a helpful contact with them? What might you do?

2. How many post–high school young single members of your church live in the area served by your church? In what ways are they active in the life of the congregation? What might your church do to meet their special needs?

3. How many sons and daughters of your members between eighteen and twenty-five years of age are not members of your church? How many have dropped out and been removed from your rolls? How many of them are still in the community you serve? What approach to those in your area might you make to meet their special needs on behalf of the congregation? What might you do to express the church's concern for those who have moved away?

4. What potential for a young-adult singles ministry is there in the community your congregation serves? What, if anything, might your church do to minister to them? Are other churches meeting their needs? If not, is there a possibility of joining with other churches in developing a ministry to them?

RESOURCES

Gribbon, Robert T. *Developing Faith in Young Adults.* Washington, D.C.: The Alban Institute, 1990.

Oswald, Roy M., and Speed B. Leas. *The Inviting Church.* Washington, D.C.: The Alban Institute, 1990.

Sample, Tex. *U.S. Lifestyles and Mainline Churches: A Key to Reaching People in the 90's.* Louisville, Ky.: Westminster/John Knox Press, 1990.

Yankelovich, Daniel. *New Rules: Searching for Self-Fulfillment in a World Turned Upside Down.* New York: Random House, 1981.

12

Enrich the Lives of Seniors

O God, I'm not what once I used to be.
I cannot always trust my memory
When it deceives and causes to forget.
Strength diminished soon runs out.
To pace myself is what it's all about.

I'll not put upon myself bitterness that lets me see
Myself upon a shelf surrounded by regret.
I can still embrace Goodness that now graces life.
I'll usher in another day, and let life come along what may.

A whole new world invisible is waiting my discovery.
Instead of clinging to the past, I'll give myself a gentle shove
To take experience new and vast, surrounded by unmeasured love.

Verna G. Smith

Aging members constitute an increasing proportion of the membership of mainline churches. In 1988, for example, more than one-fourth of Presbyterians were over age sixty-five, a giant leap from the 1973 figure of about 10 percent.[1]

All agree that the proportion of the elderly in the population will increase as years go by. This will be more true for mainline congregations than for the nation. In the general population, 35 percent is over fifty. In contrast, 51 percent of Presbyterians, 47 percent of Methodists, 46 percent of Lutherans, and 43 percent of Episcopalians are over fifty.[2]

Undoubtedly, a ministry to the aging is an important responsibility for most congregations. And the quality of that ministry will affect the loyalty of its senior citizens.

In many ways the basic needs described in chapters 3 through 6 are the same for seniors as they are for all other members of the church. Programs already described will meet many of their needs. In addition seniors have specific needs that may modify common programs or require special approaches.

155

Seniors find opportunities for fellowship in Mariners ships or other fellowship groups, and in breakfasts, lunches, and potlucks with interesting programs. Most have time for excursions, theater parties, bridge, bowling, golf, hobby groups, and other recreation. Some churches organize travel groups. In advance, seniors can study places they are going to visit.

With retirement, life patterns change. Play takes the place of work, and work becomes recreation. Meetings and fun during the day may take the place of night-time entertainment as older folks go to bed earlier or prefer not to go out at night.

Many seniors use their time in volunteer service in the community or in church-sponsored ministries. Seniors in Faith Church work in a depressed community of migrants. Forty-one seniors went to a two-week work camp at a mission school in Alaska. They worked so hard in half-day shifts that they finished the work assigned them in two days and went on to other tasks. They accomplished much more than young people had done in previous work camps.

FINDING MEANING AS LIFE COMES TO A CLOSE

As years go by, the need for meaning becomes more intense. Seniors live with increasing limitations on their physical strength and face the inevitability of their own death. The church has the important responsibility of helping people find meaning in the twilight of life. Frequency of church attendance for those sixty and over is greater than for any other age group.[3] Bible study, discussion groups, and other learning opportunities help to keep minds active and spirits alive.

Like many churches, a congregation of 230 members has a high proportion of members over fifty-five years of age. The pastor conducts a funeral about every two months. As members face death, he emphasizes that they are moving from life to life. "They need to see the hope we have in Christ," he says. "As they walk through the valley, they need to know that Christ is there. If you're going to teach them how to deal with crisis, you have to do it when they're not in the middle of it." He seeks through his preaching and through a Sunday evening Bible study group to help his parishioners find faith to see them through life's adversities. "You need to start with people where they are," he observes, "and move them where you want them to be."

MEETING SPECIAL NEEDS OF SENIORS

Life-changes bring certain needs to the elderly that are less common among younger folk. With awareness, creativity, and thoughtful planning, congregations can help meet those needs.

LIFELINE FOR THE GRIEVING. Faith Presbyterian Church[4] serves a large retirement community in Sun City, Arizona. It has designed a program for the grieving. Each Sunday underscores their loss because it is normally a family day. It is often the worst day of the week for those who have lost a loved one. By planning Sunday activities, the church provides some of the support of the missing family.

After each service, small groups of Lifeliners go for brunch together. An intensive grieving group for those with recent losses meets from two to three o'clock. A larger grieving group meets from three to four.

At four o'clock the church's four pastors take turns leading a vesper service with communion for members who find it difficult to get out to morning services or who prefer not to be out evenings. The Lifeliners then have supper together. One of the pastors always meets with them.

Smaller churches with grieving seniors could adapt some aspects of this program to their situation.

A TELEPHONE NETWORK. Many single seniors want to maintain their own homes as long as possible. When they become frail or in danger of accidents or health emergencies, they can be a worry to their children or grandchildren and to themselves. Some congregations organize a telephone communication network. Each morning at eight, assigned partners call each other. If there is no answer, an alert goes out for investigation and possible help.

A LIMITED-SIGHT GROUP. In Faith Church, a woman with macular degeneration has organized a limited-sight group. They meet on a regular basis and help people who are losing their vision to organize their lives. For example, people arrange their kitchens so they can always find things. The group is so successful that people come from other churches to learn about it.

FACILITIES AND EQUIPMENT. Barrier-free access, a hearing-aid system, large-print hymnals and bulletins help some seniors join in worship who otherwise would not be able to do so.

CPR AIDES. All ministers in Faith Church are trained in cardiopulmonary resuscitation. The church assigns members trained in CPR to provide emergency assistance at each service.

CONFIDENTIAL NEEDS OF SENIORS. The pastors at Faith Church feel a special responsibility to know what is happening with each aging member. Many have moved away from family and do not have any relative nearby to look after them. The pastors want to know whenever someone begins to fail or has some special need. Staff members enter a summary of each home visit into the computer file. Some members have no family nearby or no family at all. For them there is a confidential file containing such things as living wills, powers of attorney, and funeral plans.

MINISTRY TO SHUT-INS. Central Church, with more than eight hundred members and a large endowment, has "an intentional pastoral care ministry." It keeps in touch with members who have special needs or are going through a crisis.

About half the congregation are senior citizens. An increasing number cannot come regularly to worship services. Each member of the large board of deacons is responsible for ministering to seven shut-ins or others with special needs. Some visit every week and help with grocery shopping. Others visit three or four times a year. They make monthly reports of visits they have made and of needs they seek to meet.

A full-time coordinator of pastoral care, who also provides some secretarial services to the pastors, estimates that perhaps four out of five deacons take their responsibilities very seriously. She attributes this to the care with which the nominating committee selects them.

LINKING SENIORS TO COMMUNITY RESOURCES. In addition to the coordinator of pastoral care, Central Church employs a part-time pastoral field worker. Older members know and trust her. As a retired public health worker, she knows the community resources and can help the elderly break through the red tape, fill out the Medicare forms, and get the particular help they need.

Faith Church has a similar service rendered by a human resource coordinator. In that community this is an acceptable name for the part-time social worker who serves on the church staff.

Health insurance programs use diagnostic related groupings (DRGs) to limit the number of days a hospital will be paid for each specified diagnosis. Untimely dismissals from the hospital can be a disaster for some people who are sent home before they are ready to care for themselves and who have no one else to care for them. When a member leaves the hospital, the human services coordinator makes a professional assessment of their situation. She helps them get the resources they need and alerts the ministers to anything they can do.

SPECIAL ARRANGEMENTS FOR REGULAR PROGRAMS. Covenant Church holds its annual get-away retreat in rough camp facilities. Some seniors do not feel comfortable there. So the church arranges for nearby motel accommodations for those that request them. They also make special transportation arrangements to take seniors to Sunday worship or to other church programs.

SENIOR CITIZEN CENTERS

More than one of the bonding churches make their facilities available to senior citizen programs. Usually such programs are partially or wholly financed by government funds, serve all seniors in the surrounding area, and are nonsectarian in their approach. Ocean View Church has a senior center sponsored jointly by the city and the church. Two-thirds of its budget comes from the church, but the program serves the whole community. Unlike some centers, which have programs only one or two days a week, this center is open five days a week.

Included in its services are

an information and referral service to nursing homes in the county and to general services from federal agencies;

special informative programs titled "Durable Powers of Attorney for Health Care," "You and Your Aging Parent," "Reverse Home-Equity Loans," "The Physical Aspects of Aging," and "Earthquake Preparedness";

screening services for blood pressure, vision, hearing, and skin conditions;

a nutrition program with balanced meals for a nominal charge two noons a week; and

a driving class for older people.

There is an adjacent day-care center for Alzheimer patients. It provides supervision and hot lunches for a moderate daily fee.

DEVELOPING MINISTRIES TO SENIORS

Aging Creatively Today (ACT) is a program of Faith Presbyterian Church in Sun City, Arizona. In association with theological seminaries, it conducts seminars on aging. Seminary students come to the church for one to three weeks of instruction and experience. The congregation pays half the student's travel and houses students with its members.

Francis Park, pastor of Faith Church, expresses the hope that this program will make a lasting impact on its participants: "Never again will they allow an older person to say, 'Let the younger members do it.' (That's suicidal.) Never again will they let a young person say, 'They're retired, they have nothing to give.' (That's homicidal.)"

QUESTIONS FOR STUDY AND DISCUSSION

1. What proportion of the members in your congregation are sixty-five or older? Which of your programs specifically meet the needs of senior citizens? How many of your members are homebound or find it difficult to attend church? In what ways does your church minister to them? What else might you be doing?

2. What proportion of the population in the area served by your congregation is sixty-five or over? To what extent are other churches or community-based programs meeting their needs? What might your church do to reach out to senior citizens in your area?

3. What specific facilities do you have that meet particular needs of seniors? Large-print hymnals, pew Bibles, and bulletins? Sound amplification systems? Barrier-free access? What provisions have you made for emergency first aid?

4. Based on your reading and discussion of this chapter, what suggestions do you have for your congregation?

RESOURCES

Aging Creatively Today. A program of the Faith Presbyterian Church, 16000 North Del Webb Boulevard, Sun City, AZ 85351.

13

LEAD VIGOROUSLY AS SERVANTS

"The greatest among you will be your servant."

MATTHEW 23:11

Various studies confirm that pastors contribute significantly to congregational growth and member satisfaction. This in turn leads to member retention. Researchers have identified a long list of leadership characteristics that mark successful pastors. They are competent and warm. They generate enthusiasm, project hope, and "affirm personal faith and public pluralism." The quality of their preaching, pastoral prayers, and pastoral care is high. They are good managers.

Our study suggests that servant leadership is the key. Servant leadership draws members to the heart of a congregation. It energizes church members to reach out in service to each other and to the world around them.

In *Servant Leadership,* Robert Greenleaf tells the story of a band of men on a mythical journey. A servant named Leo "does their menial chores, but . . . also sustains them with his spirit and his song. He is a person of extraordinary presence. All goes well until Leo disappears. . . . The group falls into disarray and abandons the journey." Without him, the journey fails. Years later a member of the party joins the order that sponsored the journey. Then he discovers that Leo is its titular head, "its guiding spirit, a great and noble leader."[1]

Greenleaf defines a servant leader as one who leads in order to serve rather than one who serves in order to lead. Servant leadership serves the highest priority needs of others and prizes the valuable contribution each person makes to the whole. This describes the pastors of bonding churches. Servant leaders are not doormats. They are strong leaders for others.

WHAT SERVANT LEADERSHIP LOOKS LIKE

Following publication of *Congregations Alive,* we asked pastors of the ministering churches to rate themselves on twenty leadership skills. Elders also rated their pastors. We compared their ratings with a random sample of Presbyterian pastors and elders.[2] On eighteen of twenty skills, elders rated the ministering pastors as significantly more skillful than the average Presbyterian pastor. Pastors' self-ratings showed similar differences.

Through factor analysis, we found that eight of the twenty skills closely relate to each other. They cluster together in factor A, which we call "leadership in mission achievement." Six other skills cluster together in factor B, which we call "responsiveness to others." As with the separate skill ratings, elders rated pastors of ministering churches as more skillful than the average Presbyterian pastor on both these factors. Again pastors' self-ratings showed similar differences. In three conferences we discussed our findings with the ministering pastors. We then asked them what had influenced the development of their style of leadership?

In the present study of bonding churches, we asked many of the same skill questions of pastors and key leaders. In our telephone interviews and on-site visits, we gathered comments and illustrations from pastors and key leaders of the bonding churches. From all this we can describe more specific characteristics of the servant leader.

PREACHERS AND TEACHERS WHO INSPIRE

Pastors of bonding churches are preachers and teachers that inspire. Key members in bonding churches are more likely than key members in high-loss churches to feel that the preaching in their congregation is outstanding. They are also more likely to appreciate the quality of their worship services. Not surprisingly, inspiring worship services also relate positively to churches with high attendance.

Apparently, bonding pastors are inspiring preachers and leaders of worship, but *not* because of greater skill in interpreting scripture or in speaking clearly. Both bonding and high-loss pastors received high skill ratings on application of biblical and theological thought and on clarity of communication. *There were no significant differences between them.*

The differences seem to come in the intangible fervor and spiritual authenticity that bonding pastors radiate. Roy Oswald and Speed Leas, in *The Inviting Church,* call it "the pastor's ability to generate enthusiasm."[3] In our study, 47 percent of key members in bonding churches compared with 39 percent of key members in high-loss churches strongly agreed with the statement, "Our pastor generates enthusiasm for the Christian faith and the church."

The pastor of Ocean View Church feels that his role is to bring to the work of the church a positive energetic spirit. "It's fun!" he says. "Enthusiasm comes down from the top," said the member in another church. "The enthusiasm of our leadership is Christ-centered," said a member in a third.

FACTOR A: LEADERSHIP IN MISSION ACHIEVEMENT

Leadership in mission achievement involves planning, coordinating, organizing, and managing the life and activities of the congregation. It helps members be productive in the church's mission, sees possibilities for the future, and motivates others to respond to that vision. It assesses the talents of self and of others and assigns responsibilities to them with confidence that they can accomplish their tasks.

Factor A includes eight skills in order of their importance to the cluster: strategizing, organizing, guiding, visioning, focusing, persuading, delegating, identifying resources. These are leadership, executive, or managing skills.

In our current study we found that pastors of bonding churches are more likely than pastors of high-loss churches to rate themselves as very skillful to moderately skillful in developing strategies. Members in bonding churches are more likely than members in high-loss churches to feel that their pastor is very skillful or moderately skillful in organizing and guiding, in delegating and persuading. And pastors in bonding churches are more likely than pastors in high-loss churches to have had from very extensive to moderate amounts of continuing education in the area of administration.

WORKING WITH A STRATEGY. The pastor of Broadview Church believes that programs should relate strategically to next steps in a long-range plan unless they are meeting an immediate need. In retreats, church officers work with him on long-range plans. "This helps give the congregation a sense of direction," he points out. He encourages staff to plan strategically and to channel their efforts into activities that fit those strategies. Yet, he also allows them latitude for other efforts. "If a staff member wants to do something that does not fit our strategy," he says, "I permit it but explain that I don't think it's part of the strategy. If a member of the church wants to do something, I say, 'Sure'!"

DELEGATING. The pastor of Broadview Church believes in shared leadership and in delegating responsibility and authority to others. "The more you hold close, the less can be done," he says.

Another pastor says, "Ministry only happens when you give it away."

The pastor of Ocean View Church, like other pastors of large bonding churches, has three priorities for his time: studying and preparing sermons, working with the session, and working with staff. He has chosen a highly competent staff and works to build a team. He trusts them and gives them room to move with all their creativity. He knows how to delegate. The staff is enthusiastic about the way he gives them both freedom and support. One after another they say, "He models shared leadership. He trusts us and gives us free reign to do our jobs. He believes in us, advocates for us, affirms us, and helps us do our thing." He is always available when staff members ask for advice.

He puts it this way: "I don't know everything that's going on, but I'm very high on staff. I can't take credit for most of the stuff that happens in this church. My staff members know they can take risks, even fail."

Delegation, especially in a large church, requires careful coordination. Once a week all twenty-two members of the Ocean View staff meet for lunch. This includes secretaries and custodians. After lunch the program staff meets for an hour or more to coordinate their calendars and brainstorm programs or problems facing them. Twice a year, a twenty-four-hour staff retreat in midweek is the occasion for major calendaring and problem solving.

Each week another pastor meets with his ministry team for breakfast and with the entire staff after that. Whoever is to preach that week does the group Bible study.

A third pastor, in a church of about 270 members, has minimal staff. As a former football coach, he thinks of the session as the leadership team, the trustees as the management team, and the deacons as the ministry team. He is their coach.

The pastor of the hundred-member yoked Plainfield Church gives first priority to preaching. His second priority is working with the session. "I allow them freedom to exercise their God-given gifts. I am a funnel for getting resources to them, whether or not they decide to use them. I leave final decisions to them."

FACTOR B: RESPONSIVENESS TO PERSONS

Responsiveness to persons involves understanding the thoughts and feelings of others, seeing things from their perspective, accepting them as they are without judging, manipulating, or dominating them, and treating them with unconditional respect. It includes responding to them appropriately and placing them ahead of one's own fulfillment or advancement.

Factor B includes six skills, listed in order of their importance to the cluster: empathy, listening, collaboration, service, understanding individual growth, and style range. These are person-oriented, relationship, and group-building skills.

We found no difference between bonding and high-loss churches on ratings that key members gave their pastors on empathy. Pastors in both groups received high ratings. However, we did find that pastors of bonding churches are more likely than pastors of high-loss churches to say that they give very high or high priority to listening to people and responding to their needs with caring love. Their members are more likely than members in high-loss churches to feel that their pastor is very skillful in listening. They are more likely to say that their pastor is a warm and caring person.

Accepting people as they are, seeing their potential, loving and affirming them is a gift that pastors of bonding churches bring to their people. Soon after he began his ministry at Trinity Church, the pastor told the congregation that he would be spending a good deal of his time with the staff. They would be working together, praying together, and caring for one another. This, he explained, needed to have high priority because if the staff were not together in these things neither would the congregation be.

A member of that staff says, "He models ministry for us. He tells us that everyone needs to know how to love. He loves everybody and affirms people all over the place. He continually sends handwritten notes of appreciation, so we do too."

A member of that church who later organized their preschool describes her experience:

I got involved when the pastor came to me and said, "I'm teaching a peacemaking class. Will you teach it with me?" He believed I could do it! That's the thing about our leaders here: they just believe in people. Later when I organized the preschool, our pastor believed in me. He just had faith that God would take care of it. It's a miracle! Trust and freedom to move—that's it! So members trust each other. Even with people I don't know well, I know where they are in their faith, and I trust them. And I trust my staff!"

Members in bonding churches are more likely than members in high-loss churches to feel that their pastor gives very high priority to identifying and encouraging the use of members' gifts and talents. Members of both bonding and high-loss churches give their pastors high skill ratings in empowering. There is no statistically significant difference between the two groups. However, the higher ratings on listening and on identifying and encouraging members' gifts help to interpret what empowering actually means in bonding churches.

Church officer training plays an important part in bonding churches. Key members in bonding churches are more likely than members in high-loss churches to express satisfaction with those programs. And small bonding churches are more likely to have church officer training than small high-loss churches.

CONFLICT RESOLUTION

We have already seen the importance of managing change and conflict. In that connection we found that pastors of bonding churches are more likely than pastors of high-loss churches to have had very extensive to extensive continuing education in community organization, conflict management, and change agentry.

THE URGE TO GROW

It is clear from our meeting with pastors of both the ministering congregations and the bonding churches that they have a strong urge to grow spiritually, personally, and professionally. Although our study of bonding pastors did not go into this in as much depth as we did in the earlier study, I would describe both groups with the same words.

These pastors have actively shaped their own roles and pastoral styles. They are not passive dependents. The congregations they have served have shaped their ministries, just as they have helped to shape those congregations. They have given high priority to their spiritual, personal, and professional development through meditation, self-study, and continuing education.

PASTORAL FORMATION

In our meetings with the pastors of ministering churches, we explored their formative experiences. Two startling discoveries emerged. First, a very high proportion came from what they described as "caring families." Second, at some point in their lives, many had experienced ministry to their own critical needs by members of their congregations, sessions, or ministerial colleagues.

I close with a deep conviction. If pastors are to minister meaningfully to the pain of their parishioners, they must have experienced either the love of a caring home or the caring ministry of others at some point of need in their own lives. Many have experienced both.

This relates closely to the central importance of spiritual authenticity. Life and witness must be congruent. This cannot be overemphasized. The pastors who serve the congregations in both our studies are impressive in their authenticity as persons. Willingly they own their vulnerability as human beings. Enthusiastically they share their faith as growing Christians. Authenticity comes out of the crucible of living by grace.

Henri Nouwen speaks of wounded healers. They draw upon resources that enable them to care for their own wounds as well as the wounds of others. They make of their own wounds a major source of power. They have entered into the vulnerabilities of their fellow human beings. Through pain and self-denial, they have been willing and able to articulate their faith in such a way that it is available to those they serve. They have entered "the promised but dangerous land" and can thus tell those who are afraid what they have seen, heard, and touched.[4]

QUESTIONS FOR STUDY AND DISCUSSION

1. Do you agree that servant leadership, as defined in this chapter, is a style that can be effective in your congregation? If not, why not? If so, how can pastor(s) and church officers work together to develop that style in their mutual ministries?

2. Every pastor has different gifts. No pastor can be equally skillful in all the areas described in this chapter. It is unfair for a congregation to expect that. How can your church staff and leadership share in the tasks of ministry so as to free your pastor to make use of her/his greatest skills?

3. What opportunities does your congregation give to your pastor for spiritual renewal and continuing education? Do you provide enough study leave time and money to make this possible? What else might you do to help your pastor's desire to grow?

4. What opportunities for church officer training does your congregation provide? How can the leadership of your church grow into more effective servant leaders who lead in order to serve?

RESOURCES

Church Vocations Ministry Unit. Toward Improvement of Ministry series. Presbyterian Church (U.S.A.), 100 Witherspoon Street, Louisville, KY 40202–1396.

Smith, Donald P. *Congregations Alive*. Philadelphia: Westminster Press, 1981.

NOTES

PREFACE

1. Data for *Congregations Alive* was secured in the April 1979 Presbyterian Panel. The panel is a scientifically designed random sample frequently used to survey opinions of pastors, elders, and members of the Presbyterian Church (U.S.A.). For more information contact The Office of Research, Presbyterian Church (U.S.A.), 100 Witherspoon Street, Louisville, KY 40202-1396.

2. Donald P. Smith, "Closing the Back Door," in *The Mainstream Protestant "Decline": The Presbyterian Pattern,* ed. Milton J Coalter, John M. Mulder, and Louis B. Weeks (Louisville, Ky.: Westminster/John Knox Press, 1990), 86–101.

3. An unpublished paper, "The Retention and Involvement of Presbyterian Church Members," summarizes the statistical data from the study. It was prepared by the author as a report to the Evangelism and Church Development Ministry Unit, Presbyterian Church (U.S.A.). Copies were made available to that unit and to the Office of Research.

4. *Membership Trends in the United Presbyterian Church in the U.S.A.,* A Research Report Prepared by the Special Committee of the General Assembly Mission Council to Study Church Membership Trends, 1976.

5. Peter L Benson and Carolyn H. Eklin, *Effective Christian Education: A National Study of Protestant Congregations—A Summary Report on Faith, Loyalty, and Congregational Life* (Minneapolis: Search Institute, 1990), 9.

6. Ibid., 42.

INTRODUCTION

1. Lewis Carroll, *Through the Looking-Glass* (New York: St. Martin's Press, 1977), 44.

2. Report of the General Assembly Task Force on Church Membership

Growth, *Minutes 203rd General Assembly, 1991, Part 1 Journal* (Louisville, Ky.: Presbyterian Church (U.S.A.), 1991), 446.

2. MEET DIVERSE NEEDS

1. Lyle E. Schaller, *Assimilating New Members* (Nashville: Abingdon Press, 1978), 79–80.

2. Benson and Eklin, *Effective Christian Education,* 54.

3. David S. Steward, "Why Do People Congregate?" in *Congregations: Their Power to Form and Transform,* ed. C. Ellis Nelson (Atlanta: John Knox Press, 1988), 82, 84.

4. John Ackerman, "Cherishing Our Differences: Personality Types in the Church," *Action Information* 12, no. 2 (March/April 1986): 17. Published by the Alban Institute.

5. John S. Savage, *Why Active Members Stay Active* (Reynoldsburg, Ohio: L.E.A.D. Consultants, Inc., 1987), videotape. For an overview of issues related to this subject, see the symposium in Kenneth Stokes, *Faith Development in the Adult Life Cycle* (New York, Chicago, Los Angeles: W. H. Sadlier, 1982).

6. Warren J. Hartman, *Membership Trends: A Study of Decline and Growth in the United Methodist Church 1949–1975* (Nashville: Discipleship Resources, 1976), 46–47. In a later work, Hartman revised his five audiences to fellowship, traditionalists, study, social action and multiple interest group. See Warren J. Hartman, *Five Audiences: Identifying Groups in Your Church,* in Creative Leadership Series, ed. Lyle E. Schaller (Nashville: Abingdon Press, 1987).

3. CULTIVATE CARING COMMUNITIES

1. Douglas A. Walrath, "Why Some People Go Back to Church," *Review of Religious Research* 21, no. 4 (Supplement, 1980): 471.

2. From the statement of purpose of the National Presbyterian Mariners in an introductory leaflet dated August 1990. A revised statement of purpose is being developed.

3. Benson and Eklin, *Effective Christian Education,* 66.

4. Henri J. M. Nouwen, *The Wounded Healer: Ministry in Contemporary Society* (Garden City, N.Y.: Doubleday & Co., 1972), 93.

4. HELP MEMBERS FIND MEANING FOR LIVING

1. This interpretation was written by Avis C. Fleckenstein, director of Christian education and music, First Presbyterian Church, Ramsey, New Jersey.
2. Benson and Elkin, *Effective Christian Education,* 9–10.
3. Ibid., 16.
4. Ibid., 42.
5. Ibid., 54.
6. Lyle Schaller, *Assimilating New Members,* 100.
7. For a more complete description of Koinonia groups and other small groups, see the chapter on "Renewal Through Relationships" in Donald P. Smith, *Congregations Alive* (Philadelphia: Westminster Press, 1981), 82ff.

5. SERVE OTHERS AND SHAPE SOCIETY

1. Benson and Eklin, *Effective Christian Education,* 66.
2. Marlene Wilson, *How to Mobilize Church Volunteers* (Minneapolis: Augsburg Publishing House, 1983), 22.

6. INCORPORATE MEMBERS DILIGENTLY

1. Schaller, *Assimilating New Members,* 16.
2. Ibid., 19.
3. Roy M. Oswald and Speed B. Leas, *The Inviting Church: A Study of New Member Assimilation* (Washington, D.C.: The Alban Institute, 1990), 16–17.
4. Schaller, *Assimilating New Members,* 36–37.
5. Smith, *Congregations Alive,* 149–151.
6. Chris Argyris, *Integrating the Individual and the Organization* (New York: John Wiley & Sons, 1964).

7. EQUIP AND SUSTAIN LAY SHEPHERDS

1. John S. Savage, *Drop Out Tracks* (Reynoldsburg, Ohio: L.E.A.D. Consultants, Inc., 1987), videotape.
2. United Presbyterian Church in the U.S.A., *Membership Trends in the United Presbyterian Church* (New York: General Assembly Mission Council, 1976), 63.

3. These tasks are suggested by Melvin J. Steinbron in *Can the Pastor Do It Alone?* (Ventura, Calif.: Regal Books, 1987).

8. CHANNEL CONFLICTS CREATIVELY

1. This is the second verse of the hymn "God of History—Recent, Ancient," by Jane Parker Huber, which was written for the 1984 General Assembly of the Presbyterian Church (U.S.A.), Phoenix, Arizona.

2. Percentages do not add up to 100 because churches were permitted to give more than one cause of conflict.

3. John S. Savage, *Role Negotiation Model* (Reynoldsburg, Ohio: L.E.A.D. Consultants, Inc., 1987), videotape.

4. The "Toward the Improvement of Ministry" series provides tools for clarification of pastoral expectations and the review of pastoral performance. It is available from the Church Vocations Ministry Unit, Presbyterian Church (U.S.A.), 100 Witherspoon Street, Louisville, KY 40202–1396. (502) 569-5765.

5. Donald P. Smith, *Clergy in the Cross Fire* (Philadelphia: Westminster Press, 1973), 81–114.

6. This section on congregational corporate pain is from a telephone interview with John S. Savage, July 2, 1990.

7. Ibid.

8. Ibid.

9. Speed B. Leas, *Discover Your Conflict Management Style* (Washington, D.C.: The Alban Institute, 1984).

10. The videotapes *Coping with Conflict* were produced by the Synod of Lakes and Prairies of the Presbyterian Church (U.S.A.) and are available from the Church Vocations Ministry Unit, Presbyterian Church (U.S.A.), 100 Witherspoon Street, Louisville, KY 40202–1396. (502) 569-5765.

9. NOURISH FAMILIES AND SUPPORT SINGLES

1. The "crib connection" is adapted from the Lutheran "Proclaim" series. Crib materials are available from them for the first two years of a child's life. Contact Proclaim Curriculum, Augsburg Fortress Press, 426 S. Fifth Street, Box 1209, Minneapolis, MN 55440-1209. (800)328-4648.

2. Landon Y. Jones, *Great Expectations: America and the Baby Boom Generation* (New York: Coward, McCann & Geoghegan, 1980), 121–122.

3. Mary Graves, "Shipmates," n.d.

10. EMPOWER YOUTH

1. Benson and Eklin, *Effective Christian Education,* 43.

2. Jolene L. Roehlkepartain, *Youth Ministry: Its Impact on Church Growth* (Loveland, Colo.: Group Publishing, 1989), 4, 6, 11, 12, 23, 26.

3. Quotations from Dr. Richard Ross in this chapter are from a telephone interview with him on June 14, 1990. He is youth coordinator for the Baptist Sunday School Board, Nashville.

4. J. B. Collingsworth, "The Minister of Youth's Work with Youth," in *The Work of the Minister of Youth,* rev. ed., ed. by Richard Ross (Nashville: Convention Press, 1989), 58, 55.

5. Smith, *Congregations Alive,* 51.

6. Ross interview.

7. Mary Lee Talbot, ed., *Guidebook for Youth Ministry in Presbyterian and Reformed Churches* (Philadelphia: Geneva Press, 1988), 10.

8. Benson and Eklin, *Effective Christian Education,* 33.

9. Ibid., p. 38.

10. Ibid.

11. Ross interview.

12. Benson and Eklin, *Effective Christian Education,* 35.

13. Ibid., 33.

14. Ibid.

15. Ross interview.

16. Tapes are available from Broadman Press, 127 Ninth Avenue, North, Nashville, TN 37234. (800) 458-2772.

17. Lea Appleton, "In Search of the Small Group," in Talbot, ed., *Guidebook for Youth Ministry in Presbyterian and Reformed Churches,* 44.

11. SPAN THE YOUNG ADULT YEARS

1. This and other references to the Gallup poll in this chapter are from George Gallup, Jr., and Jim Castelli, *The People's Religion: American Faith in the 90's* (New York: Macmillan Publishing Company, 1989), 26–27.

2. Oswald and Leas, *The Inviting Church,* 6–7.

3. These figures are based on results of telephone interviews of baby boomers by a research team funded by the Lilly Endowment, as reported to the General Assembly Council Task Force on Church Membership Growth of the Presbyterian Church (U.S.A.) by Donald Luidens, 21 May 1990.

4. Robert Gribbon, *Developing Faith in Young Adults* (Washington, D.C.: The Alban Institute, 1990), 26.

5. Ibid., 71.

6. Tex Sample, *U.S. Lifestyles and Mainline Churches: A Key to Reaching People in the 90's* (Louisville, Ky.: Westminster/John Knox Press, 1990). Sample refers to the findings of Daniel Yankelovich, *New Rules: Searching for Self-Fulfillment in a World Turned Upside Down* (New York: Random House, 1981).

7. Daniel Yankelovich, *New Rules: Searching for Self-Fulfillment in a World Turned Upside Down* (New York: Random House, 1981), 3.

8. Ibid., 5.

9. Ibid., 90–91.

10. Ibid., 174.

11. Tex Sample, *U.S. Lifestyles and Mainline Churches*, 17.

12. Yankelovich, *New Rules*, 90–91.

13. Ibid.

14. Tex Sample, *U.S. Lifestyles and Mainline Churches*, 17.

15. Ibid., 18.

16. Ibid., 44.

17. Gribbon, *Developing Faith in Young Adults*, 5.

18. Sample, *U.S. Lifestyles and Mainline Churches*, 42.

19. Ibid., 34.

20. Stempler and Associates, *A Qualitative Research Report: The Peachtree Presbyterian Church Study on Single Members' Attitudes and Needs* (Atlanta: Stempler and Associates, 1990), 3.

21. Gribbon, *Developing Faith in Young Adults*, 28–29.

22. Sample, *U.S. Lifestyles and Mainline Churches*, 39.

CHAPTER 12. ENRICH THE LIVES OF SENIORS

1. Presbyterian Panel, *Background Report for 1988–1990 Panel* (Louisville, Ky.: Presbyterian Church (U.S.A.), 1990), 8.

2. Gallup and Castelli, *The People's Religion*, 104–111.

3. Ibid., 35.

4. Faith Presbyterian Church, Sun City, Arizona, has chosen to serve as a teaching center for the development of skills in ministry to older adults. Therefore we use its real name in this chapter.

CHAPTER 13. LEAD VIGOROUSLY AS SERVANTS

1. Robert K. Greenleaf, *Servant Leadership: A Journey into the Nature of Legitimate Power and Greatness* (New York: Paulist Press, 1977), 7.

2. We used the Presbyterian Panel, which is a scientifically designed random sample of pastors, elders, and members of the Presbyterian Church (U.S.A.).

3. Oswald and Leas, *The Inviting Church,* 16.

4. Nouwen, *The Wounded Healer,* 38, 84.

INDEX